My infamous roar.

With Mom at eight months.

Hanging with Dad at eleven months.

Mom, Dad, and me in Tobago, Trinidad.

Dad.

Norette's backyard, 1973.

I loved that dress. New York, 1974.

Age four—first day at Montessori school.

Age seven—hanging out at my favorite pool in St. Thomas.

Horseback riding in Puerto Rico with Terry.

St. Thomas. Fifteen. Trouble.

Italian Vogue, 1988—one of my first jobs.

In for the kill.

BIG GIRL IN THE MIDDLE

BIG

GIRL

IN THE

MIDDLE

Gabrielle Reece
and Karen Karbo

Crown Publishers, Inc. | New York

Published by Crown Publishers, Inc., 201 East 50th Street, New York, New York 10022. Member of the Crown Publishing Group.

Random House, Inc. New York, Toronto, London, Sydney, Auckland
http://www.randomhouse.com/
http://www.gabbyreece.com/

CROWN and colophon are trademarks of Crown Publishers, Inc.

Printed in the United States of America

Design by Debbie Glasserman

Library of Congress Cataloging-in-Publication Data
Reece, Gabrielle.
Big girl in the middle / by Gabrielle Reece and Karen Karbo.–
1st ed.
1. Reece, Gabrielle.   2. Women volleyball players–United States–
Biography.   I. Karbo, Karen.   II. Title.
GV1015.26.R44A3   1997
796.325'092–dc21   97-9242
CIP

ISBN 0-517-70835-3

10   9   8   7   6   5   4   3   2   1
First Edition

FOR LAIRD,
best friend and love of my life.
Thank you for all of your support and for living
your life with such passion.
G. R.

FOR KEN.
You earned your spurs on this one, Buck.
K. K.

CONTENTS

1. Enter Elvis *11*

2. Friday-Morning Grind *13*

3. The Mother Follows the Daughter *25*

4. New York *41*

5. How to Be Fabulous *63*

6. The Importance of a Door *69*

7. Suicides *79*

8. Detroit *85*

9. Extreme Femininity *101*

10. Chicago *115*

11. Big Questions *139*

12. The Saints *147*

13. The Man/Woman Thing *165*

14. Huntington Beach *175*

15. Being an Idiot *187*

16. Seaside *193*

17. Anyone Can Suck It Up for Forty-five Minutes *211*

18. Hermosa *217*

19. The Catch, the Edge *227*

20. Santa Cruz *237*

21. The Shoe Fits *251*

Acknowledgments *253*

BIG GIRL IN THE MIDDLE

Enter Elvis

ON THE BACK OF my bedroom door, in the house I lived in with Aunt Norette and Uncle Joe in Amityville, Long Island, I had a poster of my mother training dolphins for the circus in Mexico City. She is wearing a shimmery, ivory-colored bathing suit covered with pearls. It was very glam. I was living with Norette and Joe because my mother left me there when I was three and a half years old. On the day I realized she wasn't coming back—I was four or four and a half—I replaced the poster of my mother with Elvis Presley. He had his head down, his shirt open, hips forward, singing into that microphone like he was singing to a woman.

2

Friday-Morning Grind

GABRIELLE REECE LIKES TO ROAR. When she's frustrated, she opens her large, much-photographed mouth and heaves forth a sound beloved of five-year-old boys playing monster. *Errggghhhhh!* Today, at Southern California's Manhattan Beach, dressed in her uniform—black running tights, black sports top, black visor emblazoned with a white Nike swoosh—she leans forward at the waist, carotid arteries snaking up either side of her long, strong neck, clenches her fists, opens her mouth wide, and roars. Again and again she roars. Sometimes the roar is followed by a half-swallowed curse. *Farge!* Profanity earns you a red card from the ref, who gives a point and the volleyball to the other team.

Even though we live in a time when a certain amount of female brutishness is considered to be spirited and thus sexy, there are still limits, big ones. One thing women of the '90s have in common with every woman from Mary Magdalene to Hillary Clinton is the feeling that there are boundaries beyond which

you must not go or else be written off as unacceptable. To flourish personally, professionally, and, in the case of someone like
Gabby, in the public eye, you must still refrain from being too
opinionated, too emotional, or too successful. A recent cartoon in
The New Yorker shows two men at a cocktail party; one says to the
other, "She's your type. Good-looking, some money, not *too*
much ambition."

There is something you must understand about Gabby's roar.
There is nothing remotely attractive about it. It's genuine, unfil-
tered human expression. Gabby's roar—like just about everything
else about Gabby—is a shade past the pale. It's a too big sound
from a too big girl who turned bigness and buffness and brute
strength to her advantage.

Gabby's roar comes out when she's frustrated, and she's frustrated a lot these days. It's the middle of the summer, the middle
of her fourth season playing middle blocker on the Bud Light
Professional Beach Volleyball Tour, the middle of a losing streak.
Team Nike, her team, cannot seem to put together anything resembling a roll. Unlike every other women's team on the tour,
Team Norelco, Team Paul Mitchell, Team Discus, and Team
Sony AutoSound, Team Nike has never made it to the finals. Not
once.

But these are big-picture facts that Gabby tries not to think
about at 11:30 A.M. on this Friday morning in the middle of July,
round three of the three-day tournament, Team Nike versus
Team Norelco, Shoes versus Nubs. The most hazardous seconds
during a volleyball game are the forty-five seconds or so before
service when your mind can sabotage your game. When you
might, if you were Gabby, start thinking that you need a win

more than any other team, if only to prove that you're not doomed to spend the *entire rest of the season* losing. When you might start thinking how this year, more than any other, you've put it all out there. You've got the stats, you've got the awards, but this year, you wanted to both dominate the center *and* captain a first-place team. *First place,* nothing else. And there you are in fifth. Fifth place out of five teams. A bad dream that shows no signs of ending.

But you can't think that, you mustn't, and all players know this, especially Gabby. She knows that the only thing that matters is what's happening on the sand this instant. And at this instant one of Gabby's teammates, also her roommate, a quiet girl named Jennifer Meredith, rushes a shot and thwacks the ball straight into the middle of the net. Jen looks frustrated. Gabby roars; tennis great and veteran grunter Monica Seles was publicly chastised for less.

Despite Gabby's status as someone *famous,* there are not many people around to watch her play on this Friday morning in mid-July. On Friday, the day before the weekend, when the tournament is routinely crowded with the usual smacking-of-good-health-and-good-cheer California beach crowd, the scene is grungier than you might expect.

The ocean at Manhattan Beach is a disconcerting olive green, the breaking waves trimmed with pale green lace. Tiny, tobacco-colored moth flies alight on piles of kelp. Whenever the wind shifts, the tonic salt air is undercut by the carnival aromas of cocoa butter, fried foods, and incense. A blimp swims overhead. Fairgrounds by the sea.

This is the first year the Bud Light Pro Beach Men's Tour and

Women's Tour have been combined in a single event—the men's tournament alternating with the women's—which accounts for some teams having to play for whoever strolls past on Friday morning.

Sure, it seems like an up-and-running, fully operational professional sporting event; they have Smashing Pumpkins blasting from the speakers at the Sony AutoSound truck, and the giant white Paul Mitchell shampoo bottle balloon is up and tethered between two sets of bleachers, and there is a girl with neat hair posted at the Paul Mitchell booth cradling a wicker basket of sample envelopes of Super Clean Hair Gel; but the tunes are grooved upon mostly by the roadies still assembling the bleachers and the shampoo samples go unspoken for. What the organizers of the Bud Light tour have either failed to consider or didn't care to was that most people who might follow beach volleyball as a serious sport have something to do on Friday that forces them to miss the first day of play—like jobs, kids, summer school.

The pleasing irony is that this fledgling quality is what makes beach volleyball attractive; the organizers and sponsors of the sport may be in it for the usual reasons, but the players are in it for love, and for a public weary of sports as big business, it's a balm. Discovering the sport is like heading for Bali on an overbooked charter and stumbling upon a virgin beach. Paradoxically, it's both refreshing and frustrating, that in an age when professional sports are overcovered by the media, there's rarely a whisper about beach volleyball in the local paper.

It's unlikely you'll find mention of beach volleyball in the *Los Angeles Times*. Especially on this day, in the middle of July. It is

Big Girl in the Middle

July 17, a big news day sportswise, which means money as it relates to sports.

On page one, headlines: a twenty-four-year-old actor, rapper, restaurant owner, spokesman for Reebok, Pepsi, Pizza Hut, Taco Bell, and KFC, and basketball player, Shaquille O'Neal, signed a seven-year, $120 million contract with the Los Angeles Lakers. (O'Neal's contract breaks down to about $17 million a year, a million more than Lakers owner Jerry Buss bought the entire team for in 1979.) There is also an all-Shaq section: articles on The Agent, The Competition, The New Look Lakers, The Uniform, The TV Picture, Around the NBA, Assessing the Lakers, The Money Trail.

We also have the Olympics on home turf in Atlanta, where, if you believe the hype, women will figure big, particularly women in the traditionally overlooked team sports: basketball, softball, volleyball, and, for the first time, beach volleyball.

Page one of the business section has this: Some fifty advertisers have paid an average of $500,000 each for thirty-second prime-time spots during the hours of Olympic coverage. Coca-Cola will air one hundred different commercials one time each, spending $62 million for the privilege. The honor of being an official Olympic sponsor can be purchased for $40 million; for a scant $1.5 to 2 million you can sponsor the entire Bud Light Pro Beach Volleyball Tour; for $90,000—petty cash!—you can sponsor your own team.

At the back of the sports section proper, in the part of the paper that resembles the stock exchange listings, we learn that the Padres have ended somebody's losing streak and that the British Open is under way. There are smeary stats from the last Dodgers and Angels games, updates on roller hockey and arena football, bowling and minor-league baseball. Nothing about the doings of one of the most popular female athletes in America; a recent ESPN poll puts Gabrielle Reece at number seven, somewhere between Jackie Joyner-Kersee and Nancy Kerrigan.

While Shaq is putting the ink on a contract so outrageous that it inspires a reexamination of the Seven Deadly Sins, while the big dogs at Coke are mainlining Maalox, hoping their $62 million investment will pay off, Gabby is at work. Roaring and sweating and burning the bottoms of her feet on the sand—other players wear white cotton anklets or reef runners (silly looking with their body-hugging Lycra bicycle shorts and sports tops, but so what); Gabby prefers to burn the bottoms of her feet; the socks are too distracting—and losing, still losing. Gabby is at work, getting her ass kicked on a beach whose name pops up only in the "Fish Report" section of the paper.

There is no question that Gabby wouldn't prefer to be one of the much-lauded female athletes preparing to go to Atlanta. Despite the corruption of the Olympics by the market, the on-going fuss about amateurism versus professionalism that never quite rises to the level of a balls-out debate, and the tacky opening ceremonies that have come to resemble the endless opening number for the Oscars, the Olympics remain for an athlete—especially an athlete in an unheralded sport—the pinnacle of achievement.

But Gabby's game is not doubles, the game making its debut this July, but four-person volleyball, and so she is here on the beach with her team, grinding. It is Gabby's commitment for the summer, and it is part of Gabby's personal code to honor her commitments.

SHAQUILLE O'NEAL IS the new breed of professional athlete; his profession is not his sport, but creating a need for his image as an athlete who plays it. He's the guy who makes more money off his endorsement contract than he does in his sport. The kind who gets so rich he sets his family up in business. He gets his mom a TV commercial, let's say, or puts his brother in charge of his finances. He is his own corporation. The sport—the activity at which he truly excels—is secondary. It is the *idea* of him as athlete that has made him a hero. The old-style athlete is the professional athlete; the new-style athlete is the entrepreneurial athlete.

Gabby Reece is a new-style athlete. Not in the slam-dunking, body-banging, racking-up-the-stats sense, but in the multifaceted worker-of-the-media sense. In the postmodern, post-Warholian American sense. In the gorgeous, charismatic sense. In the smile-that-can-launch-a-thousand-ships sense and the strength-to-sink-a-few-single-handedly sense.

Gabby's résumé isn't all that different from Shaq's. Over the past four years she's come out of nowhere to occupy the white-hot center of popular culture, a distinguished nexus of TV, fashion, and sports. Her face stares out from the covers of a cross section of magazines that represent the new female ideal she's come to represent: *Elle* and *Outside, Harper's Bazaar* and *Shape*. At the peak of her modeling career in the late 1980s, Gabby pulled down as much as $35,000 a day. She made a hit with the Beavis and Butt-head crowd as the host of *MTV Sports,* a show that profiled the kind of eyeball-bulging pursuits that typically raise life insurance premiums, like drag racing, street luging, and skydiving.

The short-lived *The Extremists with Gabrielle Reece,* which covered the same sort of terrain, was aired in forty countries worldwide. A onetime fitness columnist for *Elle,* now a consulting editor for Condé Nast's *Sports for Women,* she is also one of Nike's marquee athletes; she was, in fact, the first woman to have her own Nike signature shoe. Hollywood has been courting her for years—offering mostly roles that feature large weapons and thong bikinis.

But Gabby—despite the cool countenance, despite the glamour oozing from every perfect pore, despite the fact she is in every way *killer*—is not Shaq. She is a woman, and she plays in what she calls "an unhyped sport."

Also, she lives by some shockingly old-fashioned principles, one of the first being that waving your tear sheets and contracts around is no form of occupation. "I'm willing to be a babe for a living," Gabby has said on a number of occasions. "I know it's part of the gig." But it's the grinding that makes Gabby able to live with herself.

For in The Gospel According to Gabby, if you don't work, if you don't grind, don't sweat or burn the bottoms of your feet, don't roar, you don't deserve to win. And it's not just that. If she, Gabrielle Reece—one of *People*'s Fifty Most Beautiful People of the Year, one of *Elle*'s Five Most Beautiful Women in the World, one of *Shape*'s buffest babes in the solar system, or some other impossible-to-live-up-to accolade—permitted herself to spend half the time basketball, football, and baseball players do being photographed behind the ubiquitous gaggle of microphones talking about her *own* megadeal (and yes, she does have one, with Nike) the world would see one thing and one thing only: a beautiful girl cashing in on her beauty.

And beautiful she is; can't say there's no accounting for taste when it comes to Gabby's looks. The square jaw, high cheekbones, and full lips that are standard issue on world-class beauties share top billing with the freckled nose, straight, sun-streaked hair, and smooth, caramel-colored skin of the most mooned-over beach babe. But there's something else going on. From certain angles, she appears vaguely Middle Eastern or African, despite her pale eyes, the startling green of a Caribbean cove. The cut of her nostrils gives her the look of a disgruntled aristocrat from one of those long-lost middle European empires that routinely conquered their neighbors and retained the musical genius of the age to play at their children's birthday parties. And then there is the 6'3", the 170 pounds—not all that much to weigh when you are that tall, taller than all but a few dozen women and most of the world's men—but still, *one hundred and seventy pounds*. And still definitely a girl.

Even so, what's wrong with cashing in on being gorgeous? Isn't it the secret female American dream? And if you imagine it isn't, there are always the results of some ridiculous poll floating around to prove you wrong. Three out of four high school girls would rather be blind than fat; the other one would rather lose a leg than be ugly. They'd all sacrifice a dozen or so IQ points for those lips, those eyes, those teeth.

From time to time people wonder about Gabby. What's . . . wrong with her, that she has to suck it up, weekend after weekend, all summer long, in a newborn sport going through the usual pangs of infancy? This very Friday night, at the ritual team dinner—even on Friday nights when Team Nike, cowed and silent from another full day of defeat, are barely speaking to one another, there is always a big team dinner, on Nike, at an Italian restaurant in Santa Monica, California, where she is Known—Gabby is asked just that—"What is it you are doing, honey?"—by the concerned mother of a Nike employee.

"Why don't you just stick to modeling? It's so much easier."

"Easier, but brainless," says Gabby.

"But volleyball is so . . . hard." Translation: Why earn peanuts getting humiliated every weekend on the beach when you can rake it in posing in front of a camera?

One of Gabby's many unseen talents is knowing exactly what to waste energy on, and enlightening someone on one of life's fundamental realities—that Difficult is inevitably more satisfying than Easy—is not worth it.

"It is," says Gabby. She leaves it at that.

On the restaurant TV, suspended over the bar, the Olympic opening ceremony plods on. The broadcast is closed-captioned, and much speculation is made over whether the captions are typed in by someone who either needs closed captions himself or by a computer not programmed to consider regional accents. Thus, *medal* is spelled METTLE, as in "the team from country X is expected to mettle"; the one that brings the house down, however, is the occasional reference to the modern Olympics, which appears on the bottom of the screen as MOD URINE.

ON THIS FRIDAY MORNING, near the end of the match between Team Nike and Team Norelco, Shoes versus Nubs, the score is 13–9, Nubs. In years past a game was played to fifteen points. If it lasted until the giant white Paul Mitchell shampoo bottle was deflated and put to bed, until all the spectators took their free *schwag*–their water bottles, miniature volleyballs, and sample envelopes of shampoo–and trudged off to look for where they parked their cars, then that's how long it lasted. This year, however, a time clock has been instituted by league officials–ten minutes for the women, eight minutes for the men. The clock is a box of long-stem roses in the ongoing courtship of television by the league, an attempt to make beach volleyball TV-friendly. For all contemporary sports, and especially the unhyped, it's a given: TV's gotta love you or no one else will.

Gabby is set the ball and she takes flight, whipping her right arm back in a move you'd need to see in slow mo to really appreciate, then smacks the ball down across the top of the net. The ball's speed and spin could knock somebody cold, but won't because it's aimed for a place near the back corner of the opponent's side; even a superhero whose superior trait was elastic arms would miss this one, but a girl lunges sideways, airborne, parallel to the ground, arm outstretched to the point of shoulder dislocation, and *pock!* contact in midair–*good up!*–the ball hurtles up at a demented angle. It should be out, but over it goes and it's in bounds and now there's Jen Meredith behind Gabby, grunting and hurling her body across the court. Another up, and back and forth the ball goes, forever on the edge of control, bodies flying, players yelling themselves hoarse: "ME–ME–ME–ME!" Or "I GO–I GO–I GO–I GO!" Or "NOBODY!" which means the coast is clear, there's nobody there to block your shot, go for the dent in the sand that'll outlast a few good winter storms.

The last brutal rally continues for a full minute after the clock expires. Team Norelco has already won the game, but Nike earns the point. It's a matter of heart and of honor, battling for the last point when it no longer matters. This is what people who love this sport love about it. The effort earns a monster round of applause from the crowd, such as it is, from the roadies and the shampoo girl, from the caterers at the back of the Invited Guests Section here to set up for lunch, from two bicycle cops who've stopped on the boardwalk to hear Gabby roar, and in the intimate rectangle formed by half-constructed bleachers and the giant balloons, the sound of the applause, unprompted, gives you goose bumps. And you understand that goose bumps, both the giving of and the receiving of, is what sports are supposed to be about. Or that's the fantasy, anyway. After the game, Gabby retires to the rear of the Players Tent and cries silently into her hands. With this loss, Team Nike's skid ties the record for the longest losing streak in the history of the professional beach volleyball tour.

3

The Mother Follows
the Daughter

SOMETIMES I THINK the only reason my mother was put on earth was to give birth to me. In some ways Terry paved the way for me. She was an adventurer. Imagine: It's 1972. A 6'2" American woman, this beautiful blonde, goes to Mexico City to train dolphins. She was a free spirit, and for whatever reason, was never able to realize her potential. I've been more fortunate, also more aggressive. In a way, Terry passed the baton to me, even if she dropped it at my knees.

Until I was seven, I lived in a small house on Long Island with Norette and Joe, the friends my mother left me with when she left. Then one day, out of the blue, she sent for me. My mother wanted me put on a plane to Puerto Rico, where she was living with her new husband. She had been gone for about four years. Norette had given me baton lessons, saved my baby teeth. Joe showed me how to put someone in a full nelson. I stood on the sofa in their tract house on Long Island, crying, "Can't you get a lawyer?" I was seven years old and five feet tall, and I was standing on the sofa weeping. I was put on a plane, according to my mother's instructions. I didn't see or hear from Norette or Joe for an entire year.

On St. Thomas, in the Virgin Islands, where we eventually settled, I wore a green plaid uniform to school. Every morning I got myself up, and then started about an hour before I had to leave for school trying to get my mother up, so she could drive me. I had her coffee for her all ready. We lived on the north shore of St. Thomas, at a ninety-degree angle off the side of the road, at a place called Carrot Bay. It was lush and hot, not sensual, like you'd expect. Not paradisiacal, not at all. We lived in a ravine.

I took walks by myself through the ravine. I was always alone, it seemed. If it had been raining, there was a little stream running through the bottom. I'd take my dogs, Lady and Felisse. They were German shepherd mixed with something else. They were mother and daughter. The mother walked behind, the daughter walked in front.

I remember in seventh grade I started having some stomach problems. I was sent to see my uncle Teddy in California. He was a doctor. He said I had an ulcer. He gave me some medication, but what was more important, he spent three weeks talking to me, and when I left I felt much better.

When I was in junior high I spent summers on Long Island with Norette and Joe, and the school year in St. Thomas. In ninth grade I went back to St. Thomas before my mother, who wanted to stay in New York for a while longer, and lived with a woman named Nanette. My stepfather sent me some money—$200—which I kept in my room. A few days after I got it I went to count it and it was gone. I was a kid for whom nothing and no one was more important than my survival. I knew my mother would not be there to bail me out if the shit got heavy. My attitude was then, has always been, if I didn't know how to take care of it myself, then I didn't know how it was going to get taken care of.

My bedroom was connected by a bathroom to the room of another woman who lived at Nanette's, and I went into her room and saw $200 sitting on the dresser and I took it. I thought, *If it's mine then it's mine; if it's not, then that's fine, too.* There was a huge drama. Nanette told me to leave, and I went to live with a friend named Johann and his mother, but I couldn't stay there too long because they lived in a very tiny place, so I went and stayed on a boat with a friend of my mother's, Gabby, and her husband, Willy. Every day I'd take a dinghy in to catch the bus to school. I was thirteen years old.

I had my first boyfriend that year. He lived in St. Croix, on another island. He was sixteen, three years and three months older than me. Scott Skinner. I still remember his phone number. I would sneak over to St. Croix. At fourteen, I was flying over and renting hotel rooms for us. Sports was not on my Things to Do list at this age; getting in trouble and driving my mother crazy was. I had no sense that my life would amount to anything at this time. I imagined I would graduate from high school and work in a gift shop.

During my junior year in high school my life changed for good. My mother decided it was time to move again. We moved from St. Thomas back to Long Island between my sophomore and junior years. I was all set to start school in New York when suddenly, three days before school is about to begin, my mother says, "We're moving to Florida and you're going to school there."

She did this so that I would have no time to launch an attack, to resist in any way. I had started to adjust to living on Long Island. I was thinking, *Okay, so I can't be with my friends in St. Thomas, but at least I'll get to be with Aunt Norette and Uncle Joe, and the few friends I still have there,* but my mother had other plans. She always had other plans.

This new school was a Christian school. All the girls here were virgins. All their parents were married. Public displays of affection were considered sinful. Where I came from thirteen-year-old girls behaved like twenty-year-olds. There are no boundaries in the Virgin Islands, no legal drinking age, nowhere you can't go, nothing you can't do. Where I came from, swearwords were used as conjunctions.

You couldn't get into my new school without an interview. A week after the semester started my mother brings me in to talk to Tim Greener, the principal. On the way to the interview I get into a fight with my mother, jump out of the car, run back to the house, lock myself in the bathroom, the whole thing. I am not in a good mood. At that time, I was so much less refined than I am now. I was brutal. When my mother finally drags me into the principal's office, I sit in the chair with my arms crossed, glaring. Then Tim Greener says, "Do you believe in God? Do you believe in Jesus Christ?"

For some reason, I really liked Tim Greener. I was

hard to handle, but when I met an adult I liked, I became very easy, very cool, no problem. Now my mother, at this time, she's been on her own spiritual odyssey. She was raised Catholic, abandoned that, then became a Seventh-Day Adventist, no jewelry, the whole bit, then embraced Christianity. I watched this whole thing happen, and it made me extremely doubtful. So I said to Tim Greener, "It's not that I don't believe in it. I just don't have any real information. I can't make a commitment to something I don't know anything about." He liked that answer because it was truthful and he let me into the school.

So here I am, the only "unsaved" person in the high school. That was my label. I was considered big and mean. I got into a fight with three girls on the cheerleading squad the first two weeks. At the first spiritual retreat I went to I was told to go back where I came from, to which I said, drop dead.

Something that I suppose was strange about me was that I never wished I was more like the girls in my school. I didn't want to be 5'3" or less forceful. Sure, it was a bummer that I could never find shoes to fit, and I couldn't wear everything the other girls wore, but I didn't really care. I didn't agonize over my size; maybe I just knew all along that it was something that would one day work in my favor. I do remember wishing I didn't have such straight hair. Back in the days when wings were popular I could never get my hair to feather. With women, it always comes down to the hair.

One day my mother took me to a Johns Roberts Powers school, right there in the middle of the mall. The woman there said, "Sorry, I can't do anything for you, you're way too tall." We lived at that time with a woman named Karol–her husband owned the circus my mother had worked for in Mexico City. Even though the woman at Johns Roberts Powers did not encourage me, I took a few classes there anyway, and while I was going, Karol decided to take some pictures of me. Eventually, she showed them to a woman she thought might be able to help me, a woman named Coral.

Karol thought this modeling was something I needed to do. I thought anything that would get me out of the house was something I needed to do. I was 6'3", playing basketball, but not really, playing volleyball, but not really. Really not happy at home, so I thought, *Modeling? Why not?* Even at that age I was the kind of person who looked at a situation and thought, *Let's just see where this goes.*

Coral gets one look at me, stuffs the photos Karol had taken into a FedEx envelope, and zips them off to

people in both New York and Europe. The next day
she gets a call from one of the agencies saying, "Send
her to Paris right away." At that time, in 1985, big girls
hadn't quite come in yet. There was Rachel Williams,
who was 6'2", and Ashley Richardson, also 6'2", then
me. Before then, models were 5'8", 5'9", tallish, but
not tall.

For a young girl then, Europe was a better place to
get started than New York. So an agent from France,
Phillipe—he's got the tan, he's got the suit—arrives at
Coral's and is starting in with the French accent when
my mother shows up and the first words out of her
mouth are "no way." She knew instinctively that this
was not right. I needed to wait. I hadn't developed any
self-discipline yet. I had focus, but mostly I just used it
to try and find ways to make my mother unhappy.
Within a year there was a segment on a highly rated
TV newsmagazine show about certain modeling agents
who were sleeping with the sixteen-year-old girls they
were flying over to Europe. One of them was Phillipe.

At school, there was one boy, a year younger, a
sophomore, completely innocent, never even kissed a
girl. Now, the boyfriend I had before in St. Thomas
was 6'3", the same size as me, a year older, very charismatic, cheated on me all the time with my friends.
Here's this new boy, 5'10" at the time, sparkling, shiny

eyes, pure as snow . . . he's the one I decide I like, Jeff Sandhoff. He came to this year's tournament in Florida, he and his brother. I had lent him money, or given him my old car a few years back, and he just sent me a check last week for the rest of it; he's very nice.

It was Jeff who taught me how to shoot baskets. His parents were wary of me. His father especially was mortified; he was a youth pastor. But Jeff was instrumental in my seeing that if someone appears good and spiritual, they might actually be good and spiritual. In his family I saw people who were very straight, and it was genuinely positive. They were a strong family, raised four good kids. Jeff's father was a person of integrity, and he started schlepping me to church every week. Part of his deal was, "Okay, son, you're going to be involved with this girl, then she's going to come to church with us every week."

So indirectly everything began shifting. It was the first time I became aware of the fact that life was about balance. I'd had so much from the darker side in St. Thomas, all the adults I knew doing XY & Z, all the kids having single parents who were bouncing off the walls, everyone having sex by the time they're fourteen. There was absolutely no balance. I was with Jeff for the rest of high school, all of eleventh and twelfth grades.

But throughout all this, I still know Coral. We stay in touch and she's still encouraging me to model. I also start playing basketball more seriously. I had an amazing coach, Dean Soles. I'd never played before and we went to the state championship finals that year. In four months he got me to play well enough to play in a state championship.

This was a huge accomplishment for him. I wasn't yet focused on sports. I was too timid to be focused. When you're 6'3" at that age, you're always apologizing for being bigger than everyone else on the team. You don't want to crowd people, you don't want to get in anybody's face. Now it's different. As an adult female I have no problem imposing myself on people, but when you're young and female and big, you think, *I just want to stay out of the way.* I also hadn't been playing, I had no real grasp of the fundamentals and so not much confidence, but people think because you're so big, you should be all-world, even when you've been playing for only three weeks. And everything was further complicated because every once in a while my mother would show up at the gym during practice and give me an ultimatum: "I won't let you play basketball until you apologize to me."

I fell in love with basketball because my coaching was so good. Coach Soles had the natural gift of get-

ting players to play well for him. At that age, in high
school, it's the coaching that's so critical. I was better
at basketball than I was at volleyball. So my stepfather
sent me to a blue chip camp, where you spend a week
with the elite of the elite, the best girls from your re-
gion come and play, and that's where I decided I didn't
want to play basketball in college—not that I'd ever
given any thought to going to college. I got five letters
after the camp from colleges inviting me to come play,
and that's where I first got the idea that I could play
any sport in college. I thought, *College. Huh.* I'd never
thought beyond high school. I got very few letters for
volleyball, however. This was 1986, going into my senior year.

During that summer I went back to New York,
where my grandmother was, and Aunt Norette and
Uncle Joe. My mother's back was bothering her, and
she told me that we weren't going to go back to
Florida, that she wanted to stay in New York to get
some medical help. So here I was; I had sort of made a
life for myself during my junior year, with Jeff and a
few friends I had made, and basketball, and my
mother says we're not going back to Florida for my senior year. I was bummed. The year before all the good
athletes had graduated and I was really the only one
returning, so the school was upset, too. The principal,

Tim Greener, Tim Do-You-Believe-in-God Greener, calls my mother and says, "Send her. She can live with me and my family until you get here." So that gets worked out, but then my mother makes me sign a contract saying that I will not speak to my stepfather because they're in the middle of this big legal battle (they'd split up in '84). So I can go back to Florida as long as I don't have anything to do with him. And one thing my mother knows about me is that if I give my word on something, it doesn't matter to whom or about what, if I give my word, I'll keep it. So she kind of put the whammy on me, and it was hard.

So I went and I lived with the principal and his wife and their two small kids for four months. I remember riding to school with him on the back of his motorcycle thinking, *This is weird. The rebel of the school living at the principal's house.*

I did well in school my senior year—which was a first. I played volleyball and basketball, which I'd fallen out of love with because Coach Soles had been fired. Now my physics teacher was my basketball coach. A very nice man, but stick with the quantum mechanics, you know? So I began playing some club volleyball, USVBA, which is what the hard-core volleyball players played after the regular school season was over in December. I played in a few club tournaments and really began to like it. Eventually, it was this: I was going to go to either the University of South Florida or the University of Tampa. Tampa had an edge, because the volleyball coach was from St. Croix and I was from St. Thomas. I was going to play basketball and volleyball, with a sort of half-and-half scholarship. I thought at that time I was going to go into business, and they have an unbelievable business school. By May or June I still hadn't decided. It was late, and I was still hemming and hawing.

So it was a Sunday, and I'd said that by Monday I would make a decision. I was playing in a club tournament that weekend in Tampa, at the university, in their gym. It's the last tournament of the year, and my mother is there. Cecile Reynaud, the women's volleyball coach from Florida State, walks in and she takes one look at my mother and says, "Where's the child connected with that woman?"

Cecile watches me play for twelve minutes, then walks right up to me, introduces herself, shakes my hand, and says, "I have one more scholarship left. Would you like it?"

I responded to her immediately. She was very direct, and I've always responded to people who are right in my face like that. I knew when I met her I was meant to spend the next chapter of my life with her. It wasn't like I thought we'd be good friends, I just knew I wanted to play for her. I took a six-hour recruiting trip to Florida State, flew up, flew back, and signed my letter of intent that week. When she dropped me off at the airport, she said, "You've seen the school, you've seen my program, I don't know why you wouldn't want to be a part of it." Instead of kissing my ass, like all the other coaches did. I was impressed.

Things started to change for me then. I changed. I stopped putting all my energy into being pissed off. Living like I did with the principal and his wife was very emotionally *un*exhausting. I had been combating my mother for so long I needed a rest, and I got it. These people were reliable. I expected them to be there and they were there. It was like that for those years with Norette and Joe. There was a base. It's that hey-it's-5:30-and-there's-dinner kind of a thing. I carried around so much anxiety never knowing—where will I be going to school? will I be late? will I have friends?—but I never showed anyone. Never.

There was also someone else who was pretty influential, my Bible teacher, Mr. Strickland. He was one of those guys who felt if you got a speeding ticket, you'd committed a sin. But he wasn't a hypocrite. Some people use the Bible as a weapon, they club you with it, but Mr. Strickland used it to show us the dynamics between humans, how it was to struggle. Once he said to me, "You know, Gabrielle, I really appreciate your honesty." I was never trying to be someone I wasn't. In that school it was a very popular thing to be "good." And it wasn't that I was so bad, it was just that I never pretended. He was influential, and I'll tell you why: I didn't believe in everything he believed in, but I trusted him. He gave me respect for both adults and people of faith, something I hadn't had before.

I've always had a very strong personality. It wasn't anything I did. At a very young age, at three and a half years old when my mother left me with Norette, I think it was sink or swim and I chose to swim, and that was that. I'm also lucky because I've always had unbelievable peripheral adults in my life. Norette and Joe, when I was small, then a couple in St. Thomas, Ron and Elise, and a woman named Connie, who lived next door, Dorothy, and my stepfather, who helped raise me. Even though my stepfather wasn't much of a disciplinarian, he was very generous. When I went to New York he gave me money to pay the rent until I could get on my feet. This is not just something reflected on in adulthood; I knew it then, too. Not every kid was lucky enough to have adults come in and rescue them a little bit. I don't know if parents are always aware of the turmoil the home environment is creating for their kids. Kids need to believe that their parents are in control. The day a child realizes that her parents have no idea what's going on is the scariest day of her life.

Now, suddenly, with my mother, there's this new thing going on. My mother has decided she wants to mother me. And I'm against it. Suddenly, she wants to cook for me. I know it's her way of making amends. But now that I'm a big girl surviving in a big way, it's like, "Terry, don't make me a salad, all right? Just get in the backseat and I'm going to take you to a really great restaurant and we're going to have a really great dinner. We're doing it my way now. We did it your way for seventeen years, now we're doing it my way."

4

New York

THE SECOND TOURNAMENT of the season is held in New York, in Central Park. It is the last weekend in May, over ninety degrees—reconfirming the suspicion that New York City has downsized its seasons from four to two: the season of heatstroke and the season of hypothermia.

Saturday afternoon on the tour is way different than Friday morning. It's a scene, of the finest hanging-out-wasting-a-few-hours-or-maybe-the-entire-afternoon variety. A bass-heavy cover version of the '70s hit "You Sexy Thing" ("I Believe in Miracles") thumps out over the loudspeakers, the bleachers are bumping with overheated New Yorkers, sticky with sunscreen, who've just come from Sheep Meadow, where it's towel-to-towel, or from in-line skating around the loop, where the skaters are as aggressive as Parisians on amphetamines. People have brought coolers—beer, sandwiches, chips—or a soft pretzel from a nearby vendor.

At the buffet in the Invited Guests Section (which the organizers of the tour pray will be filled with advertising executives, corporate mucky-mucks, marketing folk, anyone who will point a new sponsor in their direction) the flow of goodies never stops: anorectic loaves of French bread and slabs of perspiring Brie; spinach pasta salad; small, round, dense chocolate cookies that look as if they may double as fishing weights; and, on a pedestal all by itself, a basket plunged over on its side, cornucopia style, with chilled red strawberries spilling out, always spilling, always cold, even in this heat.

This is beach volleyball's New York debut, and the occasion of this match is ostensibly the donation of a beach volleyball court to the City of New York Department of Parks and Recreation from Sony AutoSound. Ten thousand pounds of fancy dirt masquerading as sand have been deposited in a clearing overhung with the branches of large old maple trees. Peculiar, to look up and see foliage rather than the familiar pale blue bowl of scoured-out Southern California sky. Any city that has the right demographics (the most common beach volleyball fan is twenty-five to thirty-four, makes more than $40,000 a year, has a college degree) and can muster up a court—be it in a parking lot, by a lake, or at a shopping mall—can host a tournament. The next unlikely stop after New York is Detroit, then Chicago, St. Louis, and St. Paul, before returning to the West Coast.

Team Nike has finished their four round-robin matches—each of the five women's teams play the others once—and, for the second time in two weeks, Nike is going to the semifinals. Gabby loafs in the stands among the other spectators. She's taken her long, straight hair out of the ponytail she wears to play in; the scrunchy has moved to her wrist. She wears a plain forest-green T-shirt—swishless—and the black Lycra running tights that are, for her, de rigueur, regardless of the heat. She's in her outgoing mode—not to be confused with her warm, friendly, and polite Nike spokesperson mode—her entertaining mode, her one-woman-show mode, her I-was-with-the-USO-in-a-past-life mode. Nike's last win was one of those come-from-behind nail-biters and she is not at all pleased, but as grousing about bad play is against her personal code—once you figure out what you did wrong, don't give the lousy performance a chance to get into your psyche and take root—she opts for an anecdote.

"Did you see me? Coming off the court? I'm accosted by these two guys, Juan and Chris, and they are the total Puerto Rican gay couple. They are fabulous looking, both of them, and they want me to sign a ball for them—one of the spendy ones—and I do. Juan says, 'Gabrielle, where's you boyfriend?' I say, 'Over there in the stands.' 'You mean that guy who be yelling at you? He yell at you all the time, man.' I say, 'Yeah, I know.' Then the other one, Chris, says, 'You are so big, man, we love you.' And Juan says, 'You are more beautiful than a transvestite.' I was so *flattered.*"

People who are privy to this miniperformance are charmed. They laugh. Gabby is one of those deeply serious people who are hilarious when perturbed.

The boyfriend who be yelling at her is Laird Hamilton, sitting on the bleacher seat behind her. She drapes an arm over his tan knee, an ugly knee, as knees go—knobby, callused, scars like hatch marks. The knee of a man who has had more than a thousand stitches in his lifetime; the knee of a world-class, big-wave surfer whose picture seems to grace the walls of every restaurant in Hawaii. And the picture always looks the same—a single bright speck on a tower of water.

Were there such a thing as a perfect match, Gabby and Laird would be it—"So, like, what are you, the perfect Aryan-type couple?" quipped an acquaintance of Gabby's, meeting Laird for the first time. They are both 6'3", with light brown hair bleached permanently blond. The jawline, the biceps, a holy commitment to two sports that will never have a Monday night network telecast to call their own. They sit together high up in the bleachers beneath the shade of the maples, whose leaves are not the usual zippy green of spring, but already bear the tragic droopy quality of late August.

Gabby likes to sit in the bleachers rather than segregate herself in the Players Tent, a good place to go to get a leg cramp worked out by one of the medical supervisors—portable tables set up at the back of the tent make it look like the operating room on *M*A*S*H*—or grab a banana or a bottle of water, or gossip with your opponents. Part of the informal nature of beach volleyball is that all of the competitors mingle in the Players Tent, the equivalent of the Yankees and the Braves sharing a locker room.

Although Gabby is aware of the importance of not holding herself apart from the other players—her fame and financial success segregate her enough—she is not eager to behave as if her sport is just a bunch of pals hanging out, hitting the ball around. "I choose to stay away from the rest of the players on the tour so I can maintain a formidable relationship with all of them. I don't like to get involved in all the *stuff.* It's an energy drain, and when you interact too much with your colleagues, it tends to get messy. Soon, everyone has an opinion about you and you have one about them. It hampers my game."

And anyway, Gabby knows that part of her duties, when she is not playing, is to make herself available. She is proud of this fact, that she takes her responsibilities as a public person seriously. "There are male athletes who land some juicy endorsement contract and then it's like, 'Hey, I'm wearin' your stupid clothes, don't bug me.' I try to represent Nike to the best of my ability. If that means signing autographs when I don't particularly want to, I will. If that means signing an extra ten so that every kid who wants one has one, I will."

So even though she sits in the stands like anyone else, there are always flocks of autograph seekers, as common as starlings, and people who want to take her picture—something she won't allow. "I'll have my picture taken *with* you," she says to a fifteen-year-old, pierced lower lip, a field of pimples on the planes of his cheeks, lowered lashes. She unfolds herself and stands beside him, drops her arm around his knobby shoulders. Prom picture grins. Laird is always the obliging photographer. By the end of the season he will know how to operate just about every popular camera sold in the country.

Since this is New York, one of Gabby's half-dozen hometowns—the childhood years spent on Long Island and the years spent modeling here—old acquaintances show up. A photographer from some magazine, an editor from another. A woman who works for a company that makes "eyewear for sports" wants

Gabby's opinion on a new product—eye protection for basketball players that looks as if it belongs on the brow of a welder. Gabby receives them all. Like royalty, she is expected to be polite. It's part of the gig. Not the gig of a famous athlete, but a famous *female* athlete. *I am a babe for a living,* and part of being a babe is refraining from being rude.

This expectation is more reliable than any win. It's always the same. Not two steps off the court, after having suffered an ugly loss, the coach is handing Gabby a towel and a bottle of water—and words about the lack of team unity, the lack of speed, the lack of this, the lack of that—and there's inevitably someone standing before her, looking hopeful, a pen dangling from her fingers. "You're my idol," says Hopeful Fan. "Will you sign my T-shirt?" "Sure," says Gabby. And she *says* it. She doesn't sigh, rarely remains mute . . . or, another day, at 7 A.M., in the gym, when she is sucking it up, deadlifting sixty-five-pound weights, there is always a fellow lifter who needs to make contact, who needs to capture her attention, or, even better, give her advice or make a remark. "You think I look even sweatier in person than I do on TV? Isn't that something? An autograph? Sure" . . . or during the Friday morning grind when she has her game face on, walking from the Players Tent to the court, ready to face a team who will most likely shut her down, there, blocking her way, is a mother with a young athletic daughter. "I'm an inspiration to you and your daughter? Sign this picture she drew of me? Sure. Of course, of course." Until death do I part, of course. The real dilemma of the professional female athlete isn't can she be masculine enough to play the sport while retaining her femininity but will she ever be fully relieved of her hostess duties? Her role as the glue of civilization? The facilitator of family and connection? Not, will she ever be tough enough, but can she ever *afford* to be tough at the price of nice?

THAT NIGHT, THERE is a team dinner at the Official All-Star Cafe, part-owned by . . . who else? Shaquille O'Neal. Gabby is dressed in a pair of tight black shorts no bigger than a tea towel, a tight white polyester blouse with a lavender sheen that resembles the scales of some kind of magical fish, white slip-on sandals, and mint-green nail polish. Almost two weeks later, before the tournament in Detroit, she will still be wearing the mint green. Team Nike did fine in New York (one of the best performances they would have all summer, as it would turn out), and she was wearing this same polish, so it would obviously be bad luck to take it off, a superstition it tickles Gabby to indulge in, since in almost every other facet of her life she allows herself no such silliness.

Some of the younger girls on the tour, who are only a year or two younger than Gabby but seem so much younger, are just out of college and have spent the hours of their short lives in gyms and on courts, in school buses and weight rooms, and have never been to New York. They are predictably dazzled, distracted. They want to go shopping. They want to go dancing. They want to run into Brad Pitt in the lobby of the hotel! And they do, they do.

And if they are dazzled by New York, New York, which may lay claim to the world's most beautiful women, is a little amazed by them. They travel in packs–5'10" and above, most of them–

wearing their shorts and miniskirts, their strong, curvy legs built on the beaches of California; quads and calves no amount of time on the StairMaster can give you; lip gloss and the hair, all of them, every girl on the tour save one, has the hair, swingy and smelling of some shampoo with jojoba or frangipani; and the polished golden tans. A player from the men's tour, who's tagged along for dinner, says, as he follows four of the girls to their table at the Official All-Star Cafe, "They are *nectar,* these women. Even more so when they're dressed up."

Nectar, perhaps, but not the ditzy *Baywatch* bimbos the stereotype stubbornly continues to suggest. Each of the twenty women on this year's tour attended a four-year college. And although half of them came from either UCLA or Long Beach State, there are players from Louisiana State, North Dakota State, and the Universities of Oregon, Texas, and Tennessee. Few of them can make a living playing beach volleyball, and in the off-season they are variously legal clerks and teachers, trainers and Realtors. A few are going to medical school.

The youngest member of the tour is Sony AutoSound's rookie Brita Schwerm, at twenty-two; the oldest is the formidable Team Sony AutoSound captain, onetime Player of the Decade at Stanford, Kim Oden, at thirty-two. There are four African-Americans, three players of mixed race (including Gabby, whose deceased father was Trinidadian), one Japanese-American, and one Latina. Contrary to the image, a measly five out of the twenty are naturally blond.

The setters, who need agility and quickness, not height, are no taller than 5'7"; the middle blockers—big girls in the middle all—

are 6'3", with the exception of Team Paul Mitchell's Diane Shoe-maker, who is 6'4". The outside hitters range from 5'9" to 6'2".

Team Nike boasts both the smallest player, Liane Sato, 5'3", 121 pounds, and the largest, Gabby, 6'3", 170 pounds (Diane Shoemaker, an inch taller, weighs two pounds less); in their elegant uniforms—black or deep green Lycra sports top decorated only with a spare white swoosh—Nike looks like a quartet of mismatched bridesmaids all being forced into the same-style dress.

The Official All-Star Cafe is stuck smack in the center of Times Square, and presumes exclusivity with the requisite maroon velvet ropes and bullet-headed, pumped-up "bouncers." The Official All-Star Cafe is to the current New York club of the minute what Epcot is to ancient Rome. Inside are visiting midwestern families, and some upstate boys having a bachelor party. Sports artifacts—a tennis dress from Monica Seles, hockey sticks from players famous only among hockey fans—are displayed on the wall in Plexiglas cases, and rock music, the same tunes overplayed on every radio throughout the nation, rumbles around the multistoried "cafe."

The purpose of Gabby's visit is to present the All-Star with an autographed volleyball. The ceiling is ringed with video monitors, and before the ceremony suddenly there appear a dozen Gabbys on the beach, smacking a ball over the net. She never watches these tapes of herself, averts her eyes instead, like the fifteen-year-old boys who seek her autograph.

Between the bar and the booths hugging the windowless walls is a small boxing ring, where these sorts of presentations are usually held. Before the emcee shows up there is some to-ing and fro-ing about what Gabby will actually do. At Gabby's insistence, the volleyball will be autographed not just by herself, but by the rest of Team Nike, and Team Discus as well. The woman who has organized the presentation wants the girls to bat the volleyball around the restaurant or maybe get a little rally going with some of the waiters.

Gabby says, "No." Not "I'm sorry, but I can't," or "Gee, I'd really like to, but it will trivialize my sport," or even "Not a chance, Jose. Would you ask Grant Hill to come here and dribble around the bar?" Famous studies of the way men and women use language have revealed that women tend to preface their opinions or refusals with explanations or apologies. Gabby does not. Occasionally an *uhhh* will slip out while she is collecting her thoughts, but otherwise she is so straightforward she sometimes seems tactless. "No," she says. Standing there in her tiny black shorts on legs that look not like flesh, but some rare, highly polished wood, and looking down, straight in the face of the woman who is organizing the event, an attractive, together woman who, next to Gabby, looks short and overdressed and overcoiffed and overaccessorized and over just about everything else a woman does to improve her appearance, and the woman actually *wrings her hands,* and says, "Oh! YES! Of course not. Certainly not. I understand. Of course not."

After the volleyball is signed and presented, kids appear from another part of the restaurant and line up in front of the boxing ring, cocktail napkins from under their Shirley Temples clenched in their fists. The MC *gushes,* "Gabrielle Reece! The top player in the league!" The rest of Team Nike and the whole of Team Discus stand beside her. They look both embarrassed and peeved.

They don't want to be up there but don't have the experience or grace to either say no or simply make the best of it.

THERE IS NEW THINKING on food if you are an athlete. Carbohydrates are out; protein is in. On the tour when the players are traveling, everything is in. These girls EAT. Gabby orders a cheeseburger and half a rotisserie chicken. She asks me to order a plate of french fries for her. "I don't want to come off as *too* much of a pig." She orders a Corona and says, "Could you bring it in a glass with a lime? And you know what? You don't even need to bring the bottle." Hip and discreet, she's always aware of her presence in public. After signing autographs for all those kids, she doesn't want to be seen swigging down a beer. Just in case. She also doesn't want to forgo the beer, doesn't want to become a prisoner of her role as a personality.

As the summer progressed, I came to understand that the seating arrangements at the team dinners were a form of communication, just as they are in nineteenth-century novels. Gabby and Laird sat together always, but not always at the head. Around them were Jane Kachmer, Gabby's manager and best friend, who accompanied her to most of her tournaments during the summer, the local representative from Nike, occasionally one or two players from another team—usually Stephanie Cox, the captain of Team Discus, also one of Gabby's friends and former teammates—and me. At the far end of the table sat the rest of Team Nike, as well as the stray family member. Tonight Gabby and Laird, Jane, Stephanie Cox, Danielle (a girlhood friend from Long Island) and I are packed into a booth; the rest of Team

Nike is sitting at another table with Gary Sato, the Team Nike coach, and Nectar Man.

It seems like two separate parties, a reflection of how Team Nike plays when things aren't going right. In the cab on the way back to the hotel Gabby says, "I felt, sitting there at dinner, like we're the parents preventing them from doing something they want to do. Like they're just itching to eat and get outta there."

Over the meal, Gabby says she is exhausted. Last Sunday, she'd finished playing in Clearwater, Florida, and flew home to Los Angeles on Sunday night, then flew to New York early Thursday morning for this tournament. On Tuesday, Gabby invited her mother, Terry, who lives in San Diego, to come for a visit.

"I thought, okay, instead of putting my mother off and putting her off, saying I'm busy—I *am* busy, it's not simply a line—I'll invite her to hang out," says Gabby. First, Terry arrived several hours late, leading Gabby and Laird to believe that she wasn't coming after all. When Gabby and Laird return home, Terry's car was there, but Terry wasn't. After about a half hour of panic, they found her in a neighbor's kitchen, having tea. Terry was also having car trouble, which demanded an extended discussion over whether the car would make it back to San Diego or whether it should be serviced in Los Angeles, and if it *was* serviced in Los Angeles, when, and how long would it take? If only a day, then Terry would simply sit at the repair shop and wait for the car, however many hours it took, for she didn't want to trouble Gabby, she really didn't.

"I'm not going to just leave my mother in gangland Venice all day, waiting while Rico Suave rips her off on the repair job," Gabby tells us. "So Terry drops off the car, and Laird and I follow her, and we get to the shop, and what do you think? She's not there. She went for a walk." Everyone at the table laughs. Gabby stares down at the remains of her cheeseburger. "You know, you try and make it funny about your family, but it's not. Not really."

All this makes Terry Glynn sound like some presenile matriarch imagined by Woody Allen, but she's intelligent, elegant, and seemingly too young to have a twenty-six-year-old daughter. An inch shorter than Gabby and somewhat thinner, Glynn has fine, symmetrical features, long blond hair, and a certain grace. Once, while visiting Gabby at home, I ran into her mother in the kitchen, peeling potatoes for hash browns. The potatoes were red potatoes, and very fresh, she could tell by their smell and texture, and we had a half-dumb, half-serious talk for twenty minutes about the joy of eating a great potato. She was charming.

According to Gabby, Terry is second in the line of tall, athletic nonconformists who make up the female side of her mother's family. Before Terry, there was her mother, 5'9" Adelaide, born in St. Louis at the first part of the century to an Irish-Catholic father who defied current thinking by insisting on education for his many daughters. In the 1930s, after graduating from college, Gramma Honey, as Gabby has always called Adelaide, or Ad, moved with one of her sisters to Santa Monica, California. At eighty-four years old, Gramma Honey can still remember the names of all the streets, although then they were dirt roads.

World War II prompted Adelaide to join the Red Cross. She was sent to Bermuda, where she met her husband, Edward

Glynn. After three children—Terry was the oldest and the only girl—Ed and Ad's marriage ended when Ad asked Ed to either stop drinking or leave.

Gramma Honey, from all that Gabby says about her, is one of those species of strong, strict, no-nonsense women who always figure as the heroines in Hollywood period pieces, whose patron saint is Scarlett O'Hara. A devout Catholic, a strict schoolteacher who never let Gabby chew gum in her house, Ad swam, grew spectacular roses, and had no tolerance for folly. She would not allow Ed to live in her house, but after a time they were able to reach an uneasy peace, and eventually found themselves getting together for bridge games on the weekend.

Terry was six when Ad and Ed called it quits, and Gabby believes this is part of her mother's difficulties. That, and the fact that Terry was more of an outcast in her time than Gramma Honey was in hers.

"Terry is the most prominent genetic freak in the family," says Gabby. "She was the first woman in our family to break the 6' barrier. At 6'2", she is taller than one brother and as tall as the other. She was extremely athletic, an excellent swimmer. I remember when we lived on St. Thomas. She'd take me to a place called Megan's Bay, a beach that was exactly a mile long, and Terry would swim back and forth across the bay for two hours. And at the end of two hours, her last stroke was the same strength and speed as her first stroke. She'd get out of the water and go, 'Ah, that was refreshing.' But swimming wasn't encouraged in her time. It was not something a normal woman did. Terry never had an arena in which she could excel. Me, I had a place, which is sports, where I could fulfill my potential. Terry was more sophisticated than Amityville, Long Island, but beyond that, there was nowhere she could go."

Where she did go, however, one night in 1969, when she was twenty years old and living in California, was a party. Where she met Robert Eduardo Reece, a graduate student from a prominent Trinidadian family. Bobby Reece was beautiful; Gabby's resemblance to him is so profound that people who knew him sometimes find it hard to look her in the eye. When he and Terry met he was in a graduate program at the United States International University, studying human behavior. His master's thesis was entitled "The Assessment of Aggressive Responses Elicited from Love-Oriented Techniques by the Children's Apperception and Push Button Tests."

On January 6, 1970, Gabby was born. Three and a half years later, Terry moved to Mexico to train her dolphins. Bobby Reece visited his daughter at Norette and Joe's off and on until 1975, when he was killed in a plane crash. Years later, when Gabby was twenty-two, she had a tattoo made on her ankle replicating the silver cross he was wearing around his neck when he died.

GABBY, DESPITE HER commitment to be accessible, is still expert at controlling what she wishes to reveal about herself, at calibrating just how much of herself to show. Even so, she continually struggles with how to talk openly and honestly about her relationship with her mother, without offending or antagonizing her, or further complicating the relationship. Even admitting that she needs *not* to talk about her mother, due to the tumultuous nature of their relationship, distresses Terry Glynn.

"My mother gets upset over things I say in print. She wants to go on and on about it and I say, 'Mom, I don't want to go on and on about it. I get it. I know it. I've been there.' I've seen people write untrue things about me in the press and I've seen people write true things out of context. I don't care. It's like when you have a terrible game, you don't want to come off the court and have people go, 'Wow, you really played a shitty game, and your team played like shit, and what about that one hit? Now that, that was really shitty!'

"I'm not saying it's not difficult and annoying having me for her child. Here I am, her kid, who was a total pain in the ass growing up, hardheaded, strong-willed, smart-mouthed, impossible in all ways, and now I'm grown up and I'm still the same and I'm admired and respected for being this way. People come up to her and go, 'Isn't it great? Gabby's so big and strong and such a tough girl!' and my mother must think, *Oh, God, I must be getting mine back.*"

Few male athletes have to cope with this dilemma—do I piss my mom off in print by being honest or do I simply lie? Even though the entire culture has been infected with the talk show–inspired zeal to get into every snarky detail of a celebrity's life, we know little about the mom of Michael Jordan or the mom of Wayne Gretzky. For all we know about Shaquille O'Neal—a full section of the *Los Angeles Times* dedicated to his *deal*—we know nothing of his mother, except that the deluge of her son's fame is so fast-moving and far-reaching it brought the chance for her to star in a television commercial floating past her front porch. (The commercial is for Robitussin, which the boisterous Mrs. O'Neal handily upstages.) In Dennis Rodman's tell-all *Bad As I Wanna Be,* where it was revealed that Rodman likes to dress up in girls' clothes, on the subject of his mother he's as reticent as a Jane Austen virgin.

It comes down to this: Generally speaking, we like our male stars for their statistics, our female stars for their stories. Marketing analysts and culture commentators alike have noted that we want to *know* about the lives of our female athletes, in part because the people most interested in female athletes are mostly women (except in the most superficial, check-out-the-pecs-on-that-babe sense), and women, forced to choose, tend to pick a good narrative over a set of fat, record-breaking stats, and in part because women look to the female athletes they revere for clues about how to be. How to train, what to eat, and, yes, how to handle relationships, including the big one with Mom.

In the Tonya Harding–Nancy Kerrigan drama-thon we heard a lot about Tonya's five-times-wed stage mom and Nancy's dear, seeing-impaired mom. U.S. Basketball Team member and gold medalist Rebecca Lobo wrote a book with her mom. It recently came to light that Olympic skier Picabo Street has taken her mom on as her business manager. Most significant profiles of female athletes never fail to mention Mom; noticing early on her daughter's unusual athleticism, did Mom steer her into ballet or soccer? Does she root her on or resent her? This summer, on the tour, there were many moms there to watch their daughters; oddly, there were many less on hand to see their sons.

Gabby's story is more compelling still. The bare outline of Gabby's childhood story, that her mother left her as a toddler to raise herself, or so it seems, with the help of a few wise, reliable adults, is like a fairy tale. Sad, yes, traumatic, yes, but also somehow magical. There was no doting soccer mom pushing her to practice at age four and a half, no dad to suss out the right coach, the best school. Already Athena-like, having risen up out of nowhere to model, then having risen up again out of modeling—nowhere, as far as the closed world of beach volleyball is concerned—to play professional sports, the story of Gabby's childhood only makes her seem more like a goddess. And not just a goddess created by another, more powerful god, but a goddess created by herself. We, who are always looking to improve on ourselves, our look, and even our game, whatever that may be, love this kind of stuff.

AT NINE-THIRTY, WHEN we leave the Official All-Star Cafe, it is still warm in Times Square. For close to twenty minutes, the party—the rest of Team Nike and Team Discus (who came in fourth and will not be playing in the semifinals) and assorted coaches and friends and Nike folk—stand around in loose circles, giggling about this and that, scheming about what to do, and wanting to do something, but not knowing what, exactly, and were they going to get a cab and go back to the hotel? Or no, was there some club somewhere? And they were jostled now and then, in the mash of tourists, and on it dragged, their indecisiveness, their giddiness, their itch to have something *up*. They made Gabby and Laird, who headed resolutely back to the hotel, twenty-six and thirty-two years old, respectively, seem like candidates for Centrum Silver. "Young in the head," Laird said once. "Part of the problem with the team is that the others are so young in their heads."

One of the things I will come to admire about Gabby is her well-developed ability to continually draw lines. "I don't go out," she says. "During the season my team will go out and do the typical things that single women my age like to do and I will seldom join them. I've always been a person who knew the importance of self-preservation, and if that means sitting alone in my hotel room, reading or watching TV, closing the door on the world, I will do it. Because I know when I need to conserve my energy, my focus, my voice."

While the rest of her team is out, and Gabby is back in her hotel room with Laird, conserving what she needs to conserve in order to play the next day in the semifinals, her image is on the local eleven o'clock news.

"A model athlete makes the scene in mid-Manhattan!" is the sound bite. The video shows her not playing, but donning the baseball jacket given to her a few hours earlier at the All-Star. "She is one of the world's most recognized faces in fashion as well as one of the world's top female athletes." They asked what she likes better—modeling or volleyball. The overasked obvious question. She says volleyball. The modeling is just a question of genetics. To which the banter around the news table goes, "Genetics indeed! Ho ho ho!"

THE NEXT MORNING at seven, my phone rings. The woman's voice is soft, a little vague. She mistakes me for Jane Kachmer, Gabby's manager, and says she is looking for Gabby. Although she doesn't identify herself, I think I recognize the voice of Terry Glynn, calling from San Diego, to wish her daughter good luck in the upcoming match. What, I wonder, is Gabby's mom doing up at 4:00 A.M.?

An hour later, I go downstairs to meet Gabby and Team Nike in the lobby, and there, perched on the edge of a Queen Anne chair, is Terry Glynn, in jeans and an embroidered blouse. I try with no luck to make eye contact with Gabby: *Did you know about this?* Certainly, if she did, she would have said something the night before. Can it be that Terry just got on a plane and flew across country on a whim? But I can't read anything on Gabby's face. She's got the grim game face on, is talking with laser concentration to Gary Sato, Nike's coach, about strategy. These semifinals are important. Last week, they made it to the semifinals only to lose. They need to win today to make it to the finals, if only for the sake of morale. The last thing they want is to set up a pattern of coming in third. And now, suddenly, here is Gabby's mother—who, for reasons that remain mysterious, doesn't make it to the game, which is a five-minute walk from that Queen Anne chair across Central Park West to the court.

The match is against Sony AutoSound, and with only 2:36 left to play on the game clock, it's 11 all. At 1:59, it's 13–11 Sony, then 15–11. Nike never scores again and the clock runs out.

Laird is sitting in the last row in the stands, forearms resting on his knees, green camouflage hat pulled low, blending in among the maple leaves. The season for big-wave surfing is the winter, when Laird's wave hits the north shore of Maui; in the meantime, he will travel with Gabby, offering every kind of support a man this smitten can possibly imagine. He is frustrated and sullen.

I ask him, "What happened?"

"Gab's mom showed up. And her team didn't."

BACK AT THE HOTEL, Jane and I call Gabby from the house phone in the lobby. Gabby tells us that in order to ensure some much-needed alone time, she's taken her name off the hotel register. "Is that too brutal, do you think?" she asks in a rare moment of self-doubt. She doesn't think the loss has much to do with Terry's surprise visit. "I focused on not letting her presence get to me. However, I did know what would send me over the edge—if I'd had to collect one of my teammates because my mom had apprehended her and was talking her ear off. THAT would make me lose focus. I pulled Gary aside and said, 'Do not let my mother corner any of our players.' I wish I could say that her presence was the reason I didn't play as well, but I don't believe that's it.

"I felt the team playing with me until eleven points, then suddenly they folded all around me, I could feel it. But in fairness to them, with the exception of Liane, who is more experienced than even I am, the other two are glad just to be here. They don't know that there is a higher level of play. This is a situation unique to evolving sports like beach volleyball. When a boy plays basketball in high school, he has a pretty good notion—or at least he imagines he does—of the caliber of play expected of him in college; likewise, the college player has an idea of what will be expected of him in the pros, should he make it that far. But at this moment in beach volleyball, the standards of the sport are being set as we speak. My younger players don't have a whole roster of girls they can aspire to be like. Who's the best player in our league? Does anyone know? Right now, the young ones are trying not to make mistakes. It doesn't make for aggressive play. You're not going to stick your neck out and make a big play if you worry that it may result in your being cut."

That afternoon, instead of returning to the park to watch the women's finals, taped by ESPN for broadcast on some distant, irrelevant date, Gabby and Laird catch a late matinee showing of *Welcome to the Dollhouse,* the agonizing story of a geeky twelve-year-old girl who barely survives the hell of junior high.

5

How to Be
Fabulous

BEAUTY WILL NEVER be an issue for men. No
one says, "Look at [basketball star] David Robinson
. . . he's gotten where he's gotten because he's a good-
looking man." Or what about female commentators?
"God, look at her . . . she's kind of fat." Or "She's old."
And then you get these bald guys who've been doing
Monday Night Football for the last twenty years and
it's "Hey, isn't he great?" For women, it will always be
about their looks. Always. Every great actress has an
attractiveness about her. And the big stars—Demi
Moore, Julia Roberts, Michelle Pfeiffer—aren't just attractive, they're beautiful. Then men. Can we talk
about Tommy Lee Jones? He's a great actor because
he's a great talent, period.

Sometimes on TV I don't wear any makeup and I

think, *Someday I'm going to be forty and I'm going to have to start wearing makeup or do something.* I can't stand that I'm thinking, *Well, I can get* away with it *for a few more years.* It flies in the face of what I believe about the beauty myth. I've been around beautiful women, lots of them, and it's such limited power, just being beautiful. It's not simply beauty that's skin deep, but the power of it as well. Sure, women who are beautiful have more opportunities than women who aren't, but if they have no other side to them, they're bound to fail. Beauty, attractiveness, sexiness, whatever, can only open the door.

So what is attractive? Some of the sexiest women around are flat-chested. Getting breast implants is like announcing to the world: One of the things that is most feminine about me I can't stand. To me, that attitude is less attractive than having small breasts. It's an instant turnoff, a woman giving off a vibe that says "I hate the way I look" or "I'm really unhappy with who I am."

People say I can afford to have this attitude because I look the way I do, flat-chested and all. But it's only been recently—say, in the last five years—that people have been saying, "Oh, Gabrielle, you're so *fabulous,* you're so *beautiful.*" Until then, from the time I was 5' tall at age seven, from the time I was in sixth grade and

I was so tall people confused me with a teacher, "Excuse me, ma'am, could you tell me where the science class is?", throughout the years of "Hey, Daddy Long Legs!" and "Hey, Jolly Green Giant!", I was a complete outsider.

I still have to deal with this. Once, when I was at the airport, standing in line at the metal detector, three teenagers recognized me, and whispered loudly, "Isn't that Gabrielle Reece?" (Not only am I tall, I'm deaf, too.) And I waited for the inevitable "Can I have your autograph?" This time it took a little longer than usual. One of the girls, who was standing a foot in front of me, desperate to get a look at me, whirled around and goes, "Where is she?" She's wearing a baseball cap, this girl, and she's about a foot shorter than I am. She's staring directly into my chest, and she still can't see me.

Attractiveness is all in your way of being. Men who are not handsome can still be terribly sexy. Look at someone like Harrison Ford. Is he a classically good-looking guy? Not really. But does he give off the vibe that he feels really good about himself? Yes. And is this sexy? Absolutely. There is no difference between men and women on this. Even though men get away with looking older—"He's fifty, but look how regal and authoritative he is!"—it doesn't change the reality that how you exist in yourself, in your womanliness, determines your sex appeal. Jeanne Moreau. How old is she? Sixty? Is she not sexy?

I'll never be like that, because I've got too much masculine stuff going on. But check out a woman like Lauren Bacall. She doesn't wear much makeup, she's got her hair nice, wears these killer suits, and has this great, deep voice, and she's got something to say. And she still *laughs*. You're going to tell me she's not appealing?

And anyway, why does she need to be considered desirable to a twenty-five-year-old man? She has no use for that. Forty-year-old women, fifty-year-old women—why do they care what some twenty-five-year-old guy thinks? A forty-five-year-old woman who takes care of herself, who feels good, and who has something to say is going to attract men from forty to sixty. Aren't those the men she wants to be with anyway?

Women should be happier with their looks than men because they have so many more options. When we go buy clothes we can choose pants, shorts, skirts, dresses. You got your long hair, short hair, blond hair, red hair, curly hair, straight hair, styled hair. Makeup, lipstick, blush, mascara, plastic *surgery*, long nails, fake nails. To shave or not to shave. And on and on and on.

Women just need to find out what in the hell *they* like. Certainly I try to make myself attractive to my man, but I also know what I like. I haven't changed very much over the years. I know what I look good in and what I look goofy in. I know what I am and my style reflects that.

[6]

The Importance
of a Door

AFTER NEW YORK, Gabby orders daily afternoon practices. In preparation for playing in the nonbeach city of Detroit, the team practices not at the beach, but at a family park with hard, sharp sand. In the morning, Gabby trains. Her schedule is no different from that of a grammar school child: to bed by nine-thirty, up at seven, and then to the gym. She concentrates on eating her four to five meals a day. She rests.

Between training and practicing and entertaining a friend from New York who's come to stay for a few days, she has a day's worth of work on a movie. In the movie—which takes place a few generations in the future, when people are being genetically engineered as a matter of routine—Gabby's role is as a genetically perfect fitness trainer.

The film is being shot on an anonymous soundstage in Culver City across the street from the *Baywatch* set. The day is warm and hazy, the sky the color of lemonade concentrate.

Gabby's call is for nine-thirty; she is there on time—her

mother's aversion to being where she's supposed to be when she's supposed to be has made punctuality a high priority. At eleven, she is still hanging out in her over-air-conditioned trailer, with piped-in pop music that sounds as if it's part of an airplane's in-flight audio program.

Her makeup is done; her bangs are set in hot rollers. A woman from Wardrobe blackens a thin piece of white piping that runs down the leg of her tights with a black Sharpie. Gabby has provided her own tights, since there is nothing in Wardrobe that would fit. While waiting she shows me what she's brought to read: *The Brothers Karamazov, The Best Short Stories by Black Writers,* and the recent issue of *Sports Illustrated.* "You know, I'm so well-rounded," she says in her self-mocking tone.

A minion knocks on the trailer door; Gabby is wanted in Hair. Before dashing off, manager Jane gets her to sign the contracts for the day's worth of work. In the middle of signing she says, apropos of nothing, "I love my life. I'm so glad I have a sport. It's so . . . solid. Not like this—all smoke, mirrors, and talk."

"Then why'd you agree to do this?" I ask.

"One word: Janie," she says and laughs. " 'It's such a smart script!' " she imitates her manager's enthusiasm.

"Anyway, I'm adamant about trying to find balance. When volleyball is over for me, will I have nothing? Not at all. For many athletes, when their sport ends, their life ends. They're these incredible, amazing, powerful, superhuman people, then . . . BOOM . . . injury . . . career's over. Now what? They're suddenly like a six-year-old. They have the bodies of thirty-year-olds and the brains of first graders. Yeah, they've made millions, but now they have to deal with the way life is for most people and they can't. That's why I'm always open to whatever comes my way. This was one movie role offered me where I don't have to wear a bikini and carry a machine gun."

There are five chairs in the Hair trailer. Gabby is in the second chair, her hair pulled back into a neat ponytail, part of the tail pulled up and pinned into a curl on the side of her head. One of the hairdressers takes a Polaroid for continuity purposes. The hairdressers are Southern California crones in the old model—smokers with old hands, sun-damaged faces, big who-gives-a-damn smiles. The kind of women who call you honey and you don't mind. They all look as if they've been summoned to work while in the middle of cleaning out the garage. They're as unglamorous as the stars are glamorous.

Gabby is sent back to her trailer to wait, something she isn't good at, especially when the waiting is under someone else's order. When it is her own choice to wait, that is something different.

Another knock at the door. It's K, The Important Male Star's personal trainer, with a volleyball for Gabby to sign for his sister. He's got the *au courant* Roman emperor haircut, double gold earrings, and tattoo around his upper arm. "You're a great athlete," he gushes, "a great, great athlete."

Gabby waves it off.

Later, during an endless rehearsal that is closed to the rest of the cast and crew—normally, sets are closed when the stars do a nude scene or a scene of intense emotion; this time it's closed because they are running on treadmills, a situation more vulnerable than all the rest: What if one of them trips and falls à la George Jetson?–K is telling anyone who will listen that his eighteen-year-old, 6' tall sister *worships* Gabrielle Reece.

"We're from Bumkinville, upstate New York, you know what I'm saying? They call my sister Sasquatch. They call her The Incredible Hulk. Since I moved to California I'm not there anymore to deck the people who rag on her." Has the sister found sports an outlet for her size? "She's tried, but she's too sensitive. She gets her feelings hurt too much when she loses."

Gabby appears from time to time for water or a sandwich. Occasionally she stops to say, "I gotta find something else to do in the future besides this," and later, when the day stretches on into infinity, with countless takes and the heat of the lights and the assistant director carrying on like a crabby camp counselor ("People! People! If you do not have to talk, DO NOT TALK!") and, eventually, the appearance of a cuticle-gnawing unit publicist who freaks because someone has seen me taking notes, she says, "PLEASE, Lord, let me make a lot of money in athletics."

While we wait for word that we can go on the set, crew people sit around reading the paper and eating Pop-Tarts from the Craft Services table. A woman in Hair (they are, to a one, blond, short, and round) does needlepoint, while a grip shows off his six-month-old baby.

Another actor–this one an ac-TOR–catches Gabby as she's headed back to the set for more closed rehearsing (he's one of the two dozen treadmill runners who don't have any lines and are therefore not needed) and says, "Say, haven't we met?" In another time he would sport an ascot and swill brandy in an oversized goblet.

Big Girl in the Middle

"I don't think so," says Gabby.

"What's your name, dear?"

Dear? Gabby is straight-faced.

"Gabrielle."

"Gabrielle . . ." he savors the name. "No, apparently not," then, oh so regretfully, "I'm sorry, Gabrielle."

We are finally allowed on the set, where there is constant *shushing* and grips wandering around in shorts, a piece of rope threaded through a belt loop, threaded through rolls of tape, all different sizes and colors and degrees of stickiness, strips of tape also stuck to their thighs for emergencies. One wears a T-shirt that says SURVIVOR. L.A. RIOT, 1992.

The Important Female Star, the one whom Gabby is supposed to evaluate on the treadmill and find lacking, carries around her phone, a pack of Marlboros, and a red Bic lighter. She is the industry standard of statuesque beauty, of height, if not strength. Next to Gabby, she looks like a wet terrier.

For hours, the scene is rehearsed and reblocked. A production assistant with dreadlocks strolls among the cables and klatches proffering mints and bottled water from a basket, like some nymph scattering rose petals. We've been here for four and a half hours and are yet to get a shot off.

During a break Gabby commandeers the Craft Services wagon to make Laird (who's just arrived) a sandwich. This kind of getting into it with the rank and file makes Gabby seem down-to-earth. She is. She also likes to be in charge, even of sandwich making.

By 1:45 there is finally a sense of expectation in the air. Pre–getting off-the-first-shot activity—sweeping, the sound of drilling, touching up parts of the set with paint. Everyone in the scene is dressed identically in black tank tops and bottoms. PAs wander around with Linty Liftettes.

Gabby alternately sits on Laird's lap and paces in a circle. "Are we there yet?" she says, like a kid in a car during a cross-country trip. After one shot, the unit publicist pulls me aside. I'm perched on a narrow ledge next to a short Hispanic grip in headphones, who has kindly scooted over so I don't have to stand.

"Someone told me they saw you *writing something,*" she hisses. She is slightly stooped, her chapped hands clasped in front of her. She clasps and unclasps them. She is the March Hare recast as a Hollywood professional. "This was not cleared with me," she frets. "This was not cleared with the production office. Who told you you could do this? This was not cleared with me."

I tell her Gabrielle Reece and her manager, Jane Kachmer. "They invited me."

"It's not okay. It wasn't cleared with us. I'm going to have to ask you to stop writing this instant. Stop writing, please. Now. Until I can talk to this Jane person and our producer."

"Jane should be here anytime," I say.

"This is a closed movie set," she says.

Suddenly, being treated like someone who sells belts on the sidewalk for a living gets to me. I break my rule about being compliant in these situations. "I *know* it's a movie set," I say. "I've written for *Entertainment Weekly.*"

"Oh no. Oh no. That's the worst thing you could have said at this moment."

Forty-five minutes later when Jane arrives and we are led from the set through the makeshift production offices in search of the producer (we whisper like teenage girls—We are in trouble! We're being taken to the principal's office!), Jane reports that when the unit publicist phoned her she was in a double panic: first, that she had to deal with an unapproved journalist; second, that she had overreacted by ordering me to stop taking notes and had unwittingly given me grist for a metastory on how I was thrown off the set . . . "just the kind of thing *Entertainment Weekly* likes to write about!" she screeched to Jane.

We are led to a tent set up in the parking lot behind the production offices, with a collection of sooty white wicker furniture arranged around a wicker coffee table littered with foam coffee cups.

"Ah. The gazebo," I say.

We sit.

The Important Producer leans forward and starts talking circles: "It's-the-contractual-agreement-we-have-with-the-studio-you-know-we-have-contractual-obligations-to-the-actors-I-mean-we-know-it-sounds-ridiculous-but-even-if-you-do-nothing-so-much-as-mention-The-Important-Actress's-name-and-she-picked-up-a-copy-of-the-book-in-a-bookstore. . . ."

Jane and I trade glances—*not likely.* . . .

We've explained that the book Gabby and I are writing is not about this movie, or any movies, really. It's about what it's like to be a professional female athlete, and the quest for balance in a female athlete's life. We've explained that it's quite possible we won't even mention The Important Actor, The Important Actress, or The Important Movie.

The Important Producer doesn't believe this for a minute. She launches again. "The-contractual-agreement-we-have-with-the-actors-stipulates-that-we-approve-with-them-the-presence-of-journalists-it's-our-contractual-obligation-with-the-actors. In-this-scene-for-example-you've-caught-them-at-an-extremely-vulnerable-moment."

"How so?" I ask. Silent and surly up to this point, I understand suddenly and completely why Gabby prefers the life she has now over one in modeling or Hollywood. Who could bear to look themselves in the mirror in the morning when they know spewing out this junk is what they're going to have to do that day?

"They're running on *treadmills,*" bleats the unit publicist.

"That shouldn't be any problem for people with personal trainers."

Jane reassures them again that we're not interested in their set, in their Important Movie, but the way in which fitting an opportunity to do something as demanding as this affects Gabby's mind-set, her ability to manage her energy, to find balance.

Jane says "balance" a lot.

It finally dawns on The Important Producer and the unit publicist (whose pupils are pinpricks, I notice, no matter the level of lighting) that we mean it. We don't care about their movie.

"I doubt we'll mention any names at all," I say.

"You have to clear it with us if you do."

"Sure," I say, "but I doubt it'll be necessary."

"Draft up something and send it to us," says Jane, standing.

"We might have some stills you can use," the unit publicist says suddenly, thought wheels whirring. *Oh, no! Oh, no! What if I have this opportunity to promote the movie in this book and I blow it?*

"Fine," I say.

"Some nice ones. Of Gabrielle and The Important Female Star."

"Sure," I say.

"He works very hard, our still photographer," says the unit publicist. "I'm sure there'll be some good photos."

At four we break for lunch. Gabby is there until nine-thirty that night, a full twelve hours. They want her back for another day. She considers it.

"I'm always working to know when to draw the line," she says. "This is a problem for most women, and I am no exception. I know very much the importance of closing the door, but sometimes have a hard time closing it. I'm cool, I'm human, I'm accessible, but then I have a hard time saying, no, this isn't right, or this is what I need, because I don't want to alienate people. But there are times when I have to say, you're taking advantage of me. I see so many people in the public eye behaving outrageously, and I think, I NEVER want to be like that, but then my boundaries get compromised."

Gabby says no to The Important Producer. We agreed on one day and you got one day. Door closed.

7

Suicides

THE PROBLEM WITH COLLEGE was that for the entire four years I thought I was faking it. I was athletic, sure, but I was also *so* tall. I had no sense ever that I actually knew what I was doing. I had a relatively successful college career, but I never once felt I really knew how to play volleyball. That didn't happen until my second year as a pro, until 1994. Until then I may have had the stats, I may have had the awards, but I never had the confidence.

I had a terrible time processing all the information that goes along with learning a sport. I was responsible for having my team run more suicides than any other player. Cecile Reynaud, my coach at Florida State, would say, "Okay, Gabrielle's going to go to the other side of the court and serve ten balls into the middle of the court, and if she does not serve all ten balls into the middle of the court, the rest of the team is going to run." It was like the military. Cecile liked to pick on me because I was the big girl with no real skills. If you had asked my teammates during preseason training that first year, "Do you think Gabrielle Reece will make it?" to a one they would have said, "No way."

I didn't start for my first six college games. My first game starting I'll never forget: Wherever the ball was, I wanted to be somewhere else. That was my game plan. Instead of yelling, "ME–ME–ME!" I was saying to myself, *Please,* anyone *but me.*

Then, gradually, I got into the groove. I began to learn. And then the chance to model came and—this is one of the remarkable things about my coach—she encouraged me to go. She gave me this piece of wisdom: "When you are here, you are here; when you are there, you are there."

So I spent half the year in New York modeling and the other half at Florida State playing volleyball and going to college. I would never go on a job during the season. I turned down one job, $35,000 for two days' work, because I had a game. We were playing some rinky-dink school, but that was my commitment: When I was playing volleyball, I was playing volleyball. When I was modeling, I was modeling.

I was very alone. I relied on no one. Because of the money I was making modeling, I gave up my scholarship. I was nineteen. I bought a house. I wanted roots that badly. But I wasn't really enjoying anything. I was so busy trying to be grown up and serious, I didn't understand that being grown up doesn't mean being serious, it just means making sure your bills are paid.

I had a boyfriend at that time, David, who was ten years older than I was. Because he was ten years older, he knew some secrets about life. He knew that being an adult meant capturing and protecting the child in him—that that is what adult money was for. Take care of your business, but protect your innocence, your enthusiasm, making a container for the freedom you had as a kid—You see a ball! You're going to kick it! You wind up and miss it! You fall on your ass! It's hysterical! And here comes another ball! Saving that attitude while at the same time honoring your responsibilities, that's what I learned from David.

What compounded matters at school was that I wasn't going to spring training like the rest of my teammates. Here are my teammates, college girls, going to keggers, goofing off, and I own a house, I have a career. I was not playing any ball from January to August, and then, at the end of August, I would step on the court for two weeks of preseason training, then compete from September to December. My teammates would be training in February, March, April, May, and I would be in New York or Milan. We all entered school together, eight new players out of twelve on the team, and they treated me like, "Who in the hell do you think you are? You're only here half the year, you get all the attention, but we're the ones who bust our asses in the spring."

This made me insecure. It wore on me. I'm a person who needs to work hard. I've never been the kind of athlete who can stay up late the night before a game, toss down some beers, then get up and get on the court and play the next day. And win. I'm too mentally complicated. Emotionally, I would tear myself up. I would blame myself for not doing the work that needed to be done.

A lot of this attitude comes from the fact that I was penalized in college. I would go away for six or seven months and would come back, and I would get to start. My peers tortured me. At one team meeting a girl came out and said that it was just not fair for me to start after not having put in the hours that everyone else did. And I remember thinking, *Am I getting attention because I'm good or because I'm pretty?* I developed a chip on my shoulder because of this.

But all this struggle to develop myself as a volleyball

player relatively late in life, to balance my life as a career woman/model and a college girl/athlete, made me, formed my character. And it's the same for all girls who choose to play sports. Take two fifteen-year-old girls. After school one goes home and does her homework and her nails. One goes to basketball practice and runs suicides. The discomfort inflicted on the second girl, the one who goes to practice, taps into her character, forces her to grow.

A young girl doesn't get many chances to exercise the character muscle via sports, whereas for young boys, it's part of their everyday lives. For girls, it's especially good for them to be forced to work as a team with other girls, to work together under every possible condition—winning, losing, tired, grumpy, happy. It forces them to deal with unpleasant, ungracious emotions and *get over it*. It forces girls to rely on each other. It gives them confidence in other girls. Look at my friendship with my teammate Jennifer. We had a terrible season. I was forced to get in her face a couple of times. It took a day or two for my anger and her upset to pass, but the friendship remained and remains to this day.

But the most important thing a young woman draws from being involved in a sport is that it forces her to take a stand. She becomes a willing target for people to throw rocks at and she learns she can take it—one of the top ten life lessons. I've had people trash me on television, and because I'm a woman it hurts, but it doesn't kill me. A few years ago a female commentator took some shots at me after I'd done a TV interview. The interviewer, a male, gave me a platform to sound relatively intelligent and the woman commentating the piece said, ". . . and there you have it . . . another pretty girl getting a giant endorsement contract. Why has Martina Navratilova, one of the greatest athletes of all time, never gotten a contract like this?" So I called up the woman and said, "You know, I'm really disappointed. I have the same goals you do. Just because Martina has a bigger venue, does that make her a better athlete? It's sad when a woman, one who's intelligent and cares about women's athletics, bashes another woman who's also trying to be a positive force for women in sports." The woman was tweaked. She didn't know what to say. Probably she never played sports as a girl.

8

Detroit

IF THERE IS AN EXPERT on Gabrielle Reece the athlete, it is Cecile Reynaud, who's come to watch Gabby play at Metro Beach in Detroit. Reynaud is a gym teacher in the old style, with cropped dark hair and a strong, stocky frame. She wears a polo shirt, khaki Bermuda shorts, socks, and sneakers. Her demeanor is rather modest, having evolved B.G., Before Gabby, in the days before female athletes strutted their stuff. She has been coaching women's volleyball since 1972, and says she could never have predicted Gabby's success for the simple reason that when Gabby played in college, four-person beach volleyball didn't even exist.

"Four-person ball, a hybrid of indoor six-person court volleyball and doubles beach volleyball, is the perfect arena for Gabby's talents and type of strength," says Cecile. The hard wood and strict coaching style of six-person ball was too unforgiving for her large frame; the wild kamikaze athleticism of doubles failed to work her strongest talents, blocking and hitting. In the same way Gabby was a pioneer in grafting together the once disparate careers of model and athlete, she also discovered the perfect sport for her unusual physical attributes.

"The fact that half of my body is shaped the way it is has been, throughout my life, a real source of unhappiness," says Gabby, who knows why she's so good in the sand. "I was teased no end when I was little. 'Bubble butt! Bubble butt!' In the islands it was, 'For a white girl you sure have a nice big ass!' I was so self-conscious. I'd cover myself up all the time. Now, if you put my measurements into a computer, you'd see that I'm built almost perfectly for what I do. The bubble butt is what helps get the rest of me into the air. Now, it's perfect."

Cecile says that she knew Gabby could never play traditional indoor volleyball. Besides the fact that her back and joints couldn't take the pounding, there was the question of Gabby being coached. Indoor volleyball is very structured, very regimented. Gabby needed the fluidity sand ball offers—a nice way of saying she likes to have her own way.

"She's the same way with men," says Cecile. "She wants them to run the show, but she won't turn it over to them. They have to wrest it from her hands."

"Day by day, minute by minute," says Gabby later, when I tell her about Cecile's observation.

But four-person ball wasn't right for anyone on Team Nike this weekend in Detroit. Because ESPN has deigned to televise the women's final live for the first time in league history, the schedule of tournament play has been rearranged to suit them. The usual schedule mingles the women's action with the men's on Friday and Saturday, with Sunday reserved for both the men's and women's semifinals and finals. This weekend the women play nonstop Friday, ending on Saturday morning.

Thus, Team Nike has three matches on Friday instead of the usual two. They lose all three, 15–9, 15–12, and 15–8. They find themselves in the disheartening position of being out of the running for the semifinals before the weekend proper even begins.

Cecile blames their problems on lack of team chemistry. Indeed, every time they fall behind, which they do with alarming regularity at the beginning of each game, they collapse. The setter, Liane Sato, a Bronze medalist in the 1992 Olympics and, at thirty-one, the most seasoned player on the squad, also has a reputation for being the most volatile, the most "aggro." A few missed ups, and she is cussing to herself and snarling, pounding the sand with her fists; she retreats in rage. Christine "The Rocket" Romero, the rookie, is extremely powerful–as evidenced by her nickname. Her jumping serve is so fast it makes the ball sing, but when she gets rattled, she loses her head and responds by hitting the ball harder and harder . . . and farther and farther out of bounds. Jen Meredith, in her second year on the tour, is a reliable passer and setter and blessedly even-tempered, but when Gabby starts roaring and Liane starts cursing to herself and Christine grunts and sends the ball spinning into the next city, Jen's virtues are overshadowed.

There is more, of course, than Liane, Christine, Jen, and Gabby's varying degrees of experience and ability to cope under the pressure of losing. One of the joys of four-person volleyball, as opposed to doubles, is watching the team dynamic at work.

Or, in the case of Team Nike, not work. Before the first ball was served back in May, there were already problems.

GARY SATO, TEAM NIKE'S COACH and former coach of the Men's United States Olympic Indoor Volleyball teams in 1988, when they won the Gold, and in 1992, when they won the Bronze, is Liane Sato's older brother and one of the reasons Gabby drafted Liane as her setter. Gary Sato was the first coach on the tour, hired by Gabby in 1993. Before that, true to the less structured nature of beach volleyball, the team captain was also the coach. During better times Sato, who makes his living as a chiropractor, was enthusiastic about Gabby's ability to carry a team. "Our team is always basically The Gab," he once said. "Where she goes, I go. If next year she's with Team Roto-Rooter, I'm there."

His suggestion that Gabby draft Liane wasn't as nepotistic as it sounds. If there is a royal family of volleyball, it's the Satos. In addition to Gary's impressive résumé, Liane is one of the only Olympians on the tour; in 1988 and in 1992 she played on the United States Women's National Team. In 1992, she won a Bronze medal. An All-League selection at the setter position in 1993 and 1994, she was the 1993 Defensive Player of the Year. She has been in the Pro Beach Volleyball League as long as the league has been in existence. Another brother, Eric, plays in the men's league.

Still, as Gabby is the first to admit, both she and Liane are "aggressive personalities." Even before drafting her, Gabby suspected that Liane's talents, however well-honed, might hinder rather than help; the ferociousness that earned her the 1993 Defensive Player of the Year Award has also landed her a reputation for antagonizing teammates and referees alike. Gabby also worried about Liane's ability to take hard coaching from her own brother. Still, Gabby went against her instincts and drafted her.

Jen Meredith is Gabby's good friend and roommate, and even though she wasn't the strongest outside hitter available, Gabby believed that she would fit in. Christine "The Rocket" Romero, all brawn and good intentions, was untried, as is any rookie. Throughout the season, "it all goes back to the draft" would become the mantra.

But unlike more established sports, where the players you draft are the players you're more or less stuck with, in beach volleyball roster changes can be made every week. It all goes back to the draft . . . until you release the players you initially drafted and pick up someone else. Which explains the stricken look on the faces of Team Nike when I ran into them at the Ramada Inn gift shop on Friday night

The so-called gift shop was a converted office off the lobby, a depressing display of dusty candy bars languishing in their boxes, tiny foil packets of Tylenol and Alka-Seltzer, and a wooden magazine rack that displayed not magazines but dozens of small yellow and white bags of Lay's Potato Chips, lined up with great care, side by side. It was 11:30 P.M. Gabby and Laird were elsewhere. The rest of Team Nike was in search of nail polish remover.

In the dreary neon light of the shop, Liane, Christine, and Jen, with their sleek, muscular arms and legs, their swingy, shampoo-scented hair, seemed not as exotic and bright as they had in New York, where their looks are the cutting-edge combo of butch and fem, strapping young women with no apologies for abs or pecs or biceps, who still wear nail polish. Here at the Ramada, where the view across the road is of the GM Mid-Size Car Division Technical Plant, and the guests are people who've journeyed to Detroit for a funeral or class reunion, they are interesting oddities. With the exception of Liane, who, at 5'3", is nicknamed Flea, they just looked like big, worn-out girls. Even "The Rocket," with her glistening cinnamon-colored skin, tight legs, and impressively eentsy shorts, seemed pallid and almost plain.

I said, "How'd it go today?" and they gave me a collective dog-that-ate-the-hamburger-defrosting-on-the-kitchen-counter look.

"We won't talk about today," said Gary, rolling his eyes.

I imagined that they looked so greenish, so sheepish, so bummed because they had lost; in fact, some of them were on the verge of losing their jobs.

A call the next morning to Gabby confirmed it. After too many rings for a hotel phone, she picked up. I got right down to business, for Gabby is a woman with whom you get down to business, especially on the phone. "When do you guys play?"

"One o'clock. And you should know—I'm leaving today. We got our asses kicked. I've got to get home and train. I've got to make some changes." Changes meant roster changes.

But first, Gabby's got to get up and get dressed and eat something and get in the rental car and drive thirty-five minutes from the Ramada Inn to MetroPark on the shores of Lake St. Clair, where she will play The Game That Doesn't Matter with The Team She Can Barely Bring Herself to Speak To.

Detroit loves Gabby. At MetroPark someone in the stands has a homemade butcher paper banner saying just that: WE LOVE YOU GABBY! What they love, of course, is that this famous, beautiful woman has come to their hometown, bringing glamour and sheen to an activity all but the most hard-core volleyball fans find a little curious. For while beach volleyball enjoys enormous popularity on the West Coast and in countries worldwide that boast big beaches and sports-minded citizens—Australia, Brazil, Korea, and Japan—the rest of the country views it as something of a novelty.

Like snowboarding and Frisbee football, beach volleyball is considered more recreation than demanding team sport—something a frat guy might do on a summer's day when he tires of crushing beer cans against his forehead. Of course, one look at the athletes who play beach volleyball tells you it's harder than it looks, the same way it's a lot harder to run fifty yards in soft sand than it is on a track. Unlike the regimented six-person indoor ball drilled into high school teens, beach volleyball is anarchy in motion, having more in common with something like sailing. A sand player battles multiple adversaries, her opponents as well as the elements. Wind. Heat. Sun. Humidity. The depth and quality of the sand. Coarser, firmer sand is easier to maneuver in than the fine, sugary stuff, and at the nonbeach sites where they truck the sand in and dump it on asphalt, stubbed toes and skinned elbows become a sudden occupational hazard. It's four times harder to get around in sand than it is on solid ground, requiring a beach player to have twice as much leg strength as that of an indoor player.

Even so, beach volleyball is an offshoot of a game that's had trouble gaining legitimacy in the first place. There are more-basic reasons why volleyball remains a relatively obscure professional sport, despite the fact it's one of the most well-loved, oft-played high school sports. The first reason is that it's always been a girl's game, which leads directly to the second reason: If girls can play it, anyone can play it. And if anyone can play it, then it must not be a real sport for real athletes—as opposed to, say, the much-ballyhooed gymnastics, which no one can do and which is considered to be one of the greatest female sports ever invented.

The initial idea for the game of volleyball, hit upon in 1895 at a YMCA in Holyoke, Massachusetts, sounds as if it was something born in a Hollywood pitch meeting: "tennis without rackets." Cool. Uncool were the early attempts, clunky rallies using a basketball, which resulted in broken nails, sprained wrists, and the realization that to keep the volley in volleyball, they'd need something lighter.

By 1928 its feminine appeal was sealed. "Playing volleyball requires the uplifted chest with flattened shoulder blades and a straightened spine that is an especially healthful posture for women," enthuses one 1928 rule book. Also sealed was the suspicion that you could claim to be playing volleyball while just standing on the court with a bunch of other girls taking up space. "Volleyball offers great possibilities for teamwork, which girls have, for the most part, failed to develop because so many have considered it a baby game which could easily be learned in a few minutes."

For all the optimism about the rise in popularity of indoor volleyball and the Olympic debut of beach volleyball, NBC, who televised what seemed like thousands of hours of Olympic coverage, still chose to televise the games at times convenient only for shut-ins and night owls. Indoor volleyball was tucked away in a midnight time slot, eastern standard time, and the only two beach volleyball telecasts were the men's and women's finals, both broadcast at noon in the middle of the week.

But the regular-season coverage of women's fours is even slimmer than that, making NBC's effort look like coverage of the O.J. trial. ESPN, the host of the professional beach volleyball tour, still may broadcast the women's final of any given tournament a month after it's played, at odd times of the day and night, despite that fact that both women's fours and women's doubles earn higher TV ratings than any men's final. The depressing fact remains that without adequate television coverage, a professional sport is professional in name only. Without television, pro basketball and baseball players would still be selling insurance in the off-season to finance their pro careers . . . not unlike many professional female athletes today.

And fours is a further permutation still: a Xerox of a Xerox of a Xerox. It's doubles that is considered to be the true form of beach volleyball. In an article in the *Los Angeles Times* about the difficulty of attracting sponsors to beach volleyball, fours isn't even mentioned. In an article in *Vogue* on female Olympians, beach volleyball is described as being "volleyball played with only 2 people on a team (indoor volleyball has 6 person teams)." In Anne Janette Johnson's *Great Women in Sports* only one female beach volleyball player is listed (doubles veteran Karolyn Kirby), while there are three bodybuilders, two dogsledders, and five race car drivers.

A baby game. Played on the beach. By babes. Wearing the sexiest, least practical article of clothing ever invented—the bikini.

That the game is as challenging as tennis, the beach a factor that makes the game four times as difficult as it is in your local gym, and the players favor sports tops and shorts, or tank suits, is irrelevant. The stereotype is as strong, as straight as Gabby's perfect, healthful posture.

GABBY ARRIVES WITH Laird at 11:45. She is scheduled to sign autographs at the Nike booth before Team Nike's match against Team Paul Mitchell. Laird proffers a small white box. Inside are a trio of gumballs decorated with frosting to resemble beings that exist only in the decorator's head. Gabby takes an orange one, plucks off the frosting, and pops the gum in her mouth. She is peeved, aloof, nearly silent. Throughout the summer I will continue to be amazed at her capacity for both great warmth and, to the same and opposite degree, dark-side-of-the-moon remoteness. Before going to the Nike booth, Gabby produces a makeup bag with a collection of sunscreens, everything from no SPF to SPF 30. Like a mother slightly fed up with her duties, she squirts some out for Cecile and me, even though we both say we already have some on. "You don't have enough on. I know it."

Then she stalks off, leaving Laird sitting at a patio table in the Invited Guests Section, in the middle of eating a take-out burger. "Hey! Wait until I'm done with my lunch, would you?"

She gives him a look, says nothing. He gets up and grabs her arm.

"Any lunatic could come up and stab you in the back with a pair of scissors, you know?" he whispers at her shoulder.

"If someone came up behind *me,* they would also be behind *you.*"

Laird sits back down, scarfs down his cheeseburger in a few indigestion-inducing bites, and follows her to the Nike booth.

No one expects professional athletes in more popular sports—basketball, baseball, football, and hockey—to perform the functions of celebrity before they play. They are sequestered. They are allowed their own pregame ritual, their environment is structured so that they can slip into their game mode.

An hour before Gabby plays, she is tucked into a folding chair behind a table, signing posters, signing hat brims, signing water bottles and the occasional ball. Today, the Sony AutoSound truck is parked just beside the Nike booth, and the music is live concert loud. Gabby has to yell and everyone who talks to her has to yell. A kid with zits, a crew cut, and a black ACDC T-shirt wants her to sign his forehead.

"Uh-uh," she says. "No skin."

He slinks away, embarrassed at the boldness of his request and her firm refusal. She hollers after him, "Especially because you're under eighteen. Parents! You know!" To the next autograph seeker in line she says, "If I did skin I'd get every other guy coming and going, 'Hey, Gab, sign my butt.' " The autograph seeker is charmed—Gabby taking him into her confidence this way—but this oddly brusque variety of natural warmth is merely another one of those natural abilities she has a habit of laying at the feet of genetics. After the line for autographs ends, the line for pictures begins.

ONE OF THE LONG-acknowledged tricks of winning is to play as though you have nothing to lose. Of course, this mind-set is supposed to be achieved in the face of having a great deal to lose—your spot on the team, a place in the finals, the championship—rather than simply being an accurate reflection of reality. Team Nike, having lost all three games the day before, is already eliminated from the tournament when they meet Team Paul Mitchell, Shoes vs. Hair, on Saturday morning.

Cecile Reynaud and I watch from our patio table, sweat dripping down the sides of our faces, the coma-inducing humidity made worse by our overapplication of sunscreen, which may or may not effectively shield the savage midwestern summer sun, but does provide the feeling of being wrapped in an invisible Baggie.

Gabby's duties as a middle blocker are hitting—killing—and blocking, and when she is in her game, her play reminds you of a home-run king practicing hitting all by himself: The ball is set—Gabby takes a step, a leap—she's up—she aims—*thwack*. *Set-step-leap up-aim-thwack.* Gabby can get very high in the air, the volleyball equivalent of hang time, where she can get a good look at things and decide where to put the ball. If the set is good, she can tuck a ball just inside one of the back corners, aimed between the upraised arms of two of her opponents.

Both Hair and Shoes are riled up today. There's a lot of talking back to the refs. Missy Kurt, Team Paul Mitchell's setter, gets herself a yellow card. A warning is issued by the refs that she's got to stop acting up. Then, when the score is 14–4 Nike, Kurt stomps over and gets into it again and earns a red card, which is a point and a turnover and, unbelievably, the game. It's Nike, 15–4.

Gabby bounds over to our table minutes after the game is over. This is unlike her; after a game she usually proceeds in a stately fashion from court to courtside dugout—a quartet of white plastic patio chairs, a blue and white Bud Light beach umbrella, a cooler brimming with bottles of Aqua Fina—where the team and coach debrief, to the Players Tent, signing autographs all along the way, toweling off, moving with the self-conscious composure of the always observed, the girl who loves the game encased in the adult who has become famous for being a beautiful woman who chooses to play it.

"Did you see who hit every ball?" she blurts out before she's reached our table. "Did you see who put Paul Mitchell away? I was set every ball but two, and put away every ball I was set but two."

Laird tells her she was awesome. Cecile tells her she was awesome. I tell her she was awesome. But then her enthusiasm subsides. She felt great, she *dominated*—one of her favorite words—but what about Christine and Jen? They hardly ever touched the ball, both were reduced to being diggers, two bodies on the court and maybe an outstretched arm where you need one, feeding everything to Gabby.

"One of my goals this year was to grow as a leader—if I just take over the game, then what's the point?" she says.

"But if you've got Michael Jordan on your team you've got Michael Jordan on your team, right?" asks Cecile rhetorically. "The point is to win, not make the other members of the team feel good about life. This is professional sports. The point is to win."

"If I'm set on every serve, the other team will know what's coming," says Gabby, still not quite getting at what she means.

"Who cares if they know what comes next? They can't stop it."

"But here's the thing. This morning. Woke up. I'm *pissed* about yesterday, but I decide I am not going to waste energy on it. So I was utterly silent. Did you see me? Even throughout warm-ups. Yesterday I tried to motivate them, but I'm, like, if you do something bad, you're going to hear about it; if you do something good, that's just expected. That's how I am on myself, and it's not the most supportive environment to work in. Look at every other team—they all have one player who's the cheerleader, and usually it's the captain. We don't. Somehow, I need to be more of a role model or something. But then, when I just ignore them and focus on my game, we win."

After Gabby and Laird leave to catch their plane, Cecile and I stay to watch the men play and I ask her if this is an attitude typical of women. Men, after losing a game, tend to feel (or claim to feel) that "this is a team sport," "we all worked together," etc. They don't take personal responsibility for the entire team. As aggressive and male as Gabby is in her ability to focus and compete, she still harbors the concern that the team does not fully function as a team. She does not want to be Gabby and the Gabbettes; she wants to be Team Nike.

Cecile agreed that this feeling is definitely a girl thing. Guys who are having a great game usually wish the rest of the team would disappear, whereas a woman who's having a great game wants everyone else to have a great game, too. "And Gabby has that caretaker side to her anyway," says Cecile.

Big Girl in the Middle

FEMINISTS WHO THINK about women and sports like to put forth the wishful notion that the way women play, the way they behave in team situations, is somehow changing the more brutish, warlike aspects of athletics. Author and former pro basketball player Mariah Nelson Burton, in her book whose title says it all, *Are We Winning Yet? How Women Are Changing Sports and Sports Are Changing Women,* suggests that the growing presence of women and girls in sports is replacing the ruthlessness and aggressiveness inherent in competitive sports with a more nurturing environment. Words like *empowerment, encouragement,* and *supportive* seem to wind up in a lot of writing about female athletes.

This summer, on the beach, I had the chance to watch first women's teams, then men's teams, play the same game, and I didn't notice the men being either less supportive or more savage. They were quieter on the court about their expectations of one another and less emotional when a game got close. The women, on the other hand, were more verbal, and when one captain of a losing team clapped her hands anxiously and hollered, "Come on, you guys, let's *go.* Do you want to win or not?" the tone was chiding: I know what you guys are capable of doing; let's cut the crap and do it.

It's some kind of reverse sexism we've got going here, a Victorian notion retooled for the '90s, an update of Virginia Woolf's "angel in the house"—the woman who is good, productive, virtuous, lending a genteel, civilizing influence to the home. Only the new attitude is "angel on the court," where women are presumed to bring a kinder, gentler approach to sport. Watching the girls on the beach, I got the impression they could be as warriorlike and tough as they needed to be when they needed to be. I didn't see an unusual amount of empowering or encouraging going on. They did—as did Gabby when she took over Team Nike to produce a morale-saving victory—whatever they had to do to win the game.

Still, there is no denying what Cecile calls the girl thing. Even Gabby, who can be so pugnacious, struggles with the role of emotion in team play. "As captain, I'm responsible for creating an environment where my teammates perform up to their abilities, but there's a fine line. If you have a certain level of experience and intensity and expectations, you shouldn't have to compromise those so your teammates will feel better about themselves and their level of play."

Like everything else in a woman's life, it's a continual struggle for balance.

[9]

Extreme Femininity

MY FIRST BIG JOB as a model was for my hands only—$3,500 for Cutex. It was the summer after my freshman year in college. I was eighteen years old. I once again lived with Norette and Joe on Long Island until I started making some money and could afford to move into the city. Throughout my modeling career, even when I was allegedly this hot new thing, whenever things would get slow I'd go, "Get me some hand work," and they'd say, "Oh, *no*, you can't do hands. What if people heard you were doing hand modeling?" And I said, "I don't care. They pay a lot of money." The irony of this was that professional hand models walk around all day in white gloves, protecting their assets, and I was a *volleyball* player. My hands were beat.

———

MY FIRST COVER was in 1988. At the time Italian *Vogue* was *the* magazine to be in, and here I am in an eight-page layout. They're still to this day some of the most beautiful pictures I've ever had taken of me. The photographer was Steven Meisel, the most popular–if not the best–photographer of that time, and I saw the pictures and I thought, *Yeah, okay,* and that was about it. It never really fazed me. It was simply information for me. There was no emotional attachment, no sense of real achievement.

The entire time I was living in New York, when I would walk by a newsstand and there I'd be on the cover of you name it, it was the most unremarkable feeling. It was the biggest "So?" I could imagine. People get very involved in trying to claim that temporary security and power that they miss the real power, which is being comfortable, truly comfortable, with who you are. I never stopped and thought, *Isn't this great?* For me, for my personality, it's a waste of emotion. And I'm not going to waste my emotion on transient things–they're there, then they're gone. I knew that about magazines right away. You're there, and then you're gone in four weeks. I could never let my existence rely on that. A lot of girls had the attitude "I'm in a magazine, therefore I am." In modeling it can get like that.

I don't care if someone recognizes me or not. I don't need any kind of confirmation that I'm known or successful. It really doesn't matter. Life is about looking from the inside out. How many times do people spend their lives trying to adjust themselves to fit how they appear from the outside? Entire lives wasted. If I go to a party with lots of so-called fabulous people, what is important? Is it, am I seen? Who sees me? No. It's what music did I hear, or did I talk to anyone interesting?

I also knew, with the modeling, that I was never going to be willing to commit the time. I wasn't going to go to Europe to do all the shows, where I could barely fit in half the clothes, and I wasn't going to give up volleyball to travel around, to make myself available, and go to all the parties, and schmooze up all the right editors and photographers, and be all cool, and do the right makeup and do the right hair, and wear Versace clothing in my spare time. I knew I would never do that, and I knew that meant I should stick to sports, because I knew always that volleyball was more a reflection of me.

At the same time, I was battling my religious beliefs. I was going through a guilt thing. I had been taught in my Christian high school that if you create a fantasy in someone's mind, then you're responsible for the actions this fantasy generates. By this time, by the time I was eighteen, I'd made some peace with myself, with my life, and with my mother. Before I began modeling I had been walking the straight and narrow. I'd stopped drinking, had a boyfriend but wouldn't have sex, the whole thing. But now I was in a position where I was consciously choosing to make myself an object of desire. I struggled with the idea that an opportunity had come my way, but it might not be based in good, as we assume opportunities always are, but based in evil. I tried to be smart about this. I thought, *Is this going to be better for me and my life in the long run or not?*

Volleyball is a reflection of my entire personality and modeling only reflects the so-called feminine side of me. And modeling isn't even real femininity, because there's no interaction. But I still knew that modeling would be important for me, just as I knew volleyball would. How they would work together I had no idea. I looked at both volleyball and fashion and I thought, *Well, this is a little bit kooky, this mix, but we'll see what happens.* That's another thing: I never indulge. I'm not an indulger. I don't get lost in the moment. I never went, "Ooooh, look at me, I'm a *model.*"

And I did know this. In modeling, like everything else, there is a hierarchy. There are five girls who make millions—Claudia, Cindy, Christy Turlington, Stephanie Seymour, Linda Evangelista, whoever—and then are about thirty below them. I was in that group— the girls who make hundreds of thousands, a great living, but not supermodels. I had a roommate, a very pretty girl, blond-haired, blue-eyed, who got rich doing catalogues—$1,500 a day, catalogue, catalogue, catalogue. She worked constantly. I was at $3,500 for catalogue work because I had done so much editorial, but she made more money than I did because she was always working. Editorial work doesn't pay—you get maybe $250—but it does up your advertising day rate. Mine was $10,000; my roommate's was $5,000.

Anyway, I knew then—I always knew—that I was limited. I am 6'3". I look how I look. The most successful models are beautiful, but also chameleons. I'm very specific. It's why I continue to have reservations about acting. I don't imagine I'll be able to take on other personas and be very convincing about it. Both models and actors serve as screens for the viewer's projections. If you're too much who you are, you prevent that projection. I recognized that very early. I said to myself, "Gabrielle, one thing you better face, and you better face it now, is that you are going to have to do it your way, because you will never be as successful as these girls, never, doing it their way."

I think if you're considered to be a beautiful woman, it's not as easy as people think. I can play volleyball right in front of someone—and yes, I make it look relatively easy, because all good athletes make their sport look easy—and I doubt that he or she has any idea how much work has gone into it. They think that it's somehow related to how I look. They don't understand that my body is a finely tuned machine that does something. It's functional. It's an instrument. And I'm not even talking about my *mind*. People will never get past this, and the so-called beautiful woman needs to accept it. I've finally stopped caring. I realize now that it's to my advantage. People's expectations of me are very low.

They also imagine that a beautiful woman, because she knows she's beautiful, thinks she's the center of everything wherever she goes. They're observing you, but what they don't realize is that you're getting to see them with their guard down; you are, in essence, observing them. So I'm not really bitter about it. It is what it is. The same thing that frustrates me about being considered beautiful before anything else is the same thing that's opened twenty-five other doors for me. That's the way life is. As long as the people who are close to you, the people you respect and love, know that there's more to you than meets the eye, then nothing else matters.

The fact of the matter is, even if I spend the next ten years of my life trying to prove to the public that I am a smart woman who cares more about other things than how my legs are looking, it would never make any kind of long-term change in terms of how beautiful women are perceived. By then, it would be someone else anyway. It's all utterly fleeting. Look at the magazines we read. Every six months they come out with the Top Ten, the Top Fifty, the Number One, the Best, the Only. But it was somebody else last year, last month, and it will be somebody else after you. I want to say to women, please, don't put any energy into that. In this way, modeling was the best thing that ever happened to me, because I saw this so clearly.

By the time I was twenty-one my modeling career was taking a dive. To this day people like to say I gave up modeling for volleyball, just walked away from the fame and the gazillions. In fact, people were getting tired of me. They could not understand the volleyball thing. I went to Paris once and they said, "Are you modeling for real now or what?" I had switched from agency to agency to agency. I had gone from IMG to Ford to Wilhelmina to Elite, frustrated because I felt like no one understood who I was, no one was interested in interpreting me as I wished to be interpreted.

I'm certainly not the first female athlete to publicly embrace both her female and male sides, but I'll tell you what: My modeling career was a pure modeling career. Some athletes who have gone on to model are Olympians first; their achievement in sports has put them in the public eye. My career had nothing to do with my sport, nothing. Modeling is the embodiment of what our culture considers to be pure womanliness. It's extreme femininity. So I'm that, but I'm also this.

My last year modeling I worked three times the entire year. Fortunately, I was resurrected by *Elle,* who liked to use me a lot. I was in *Elle* just about every month, but it didn't help my career that much. I wasn't working, and suddenly, at twenty-one, I had no money. No one wanted me anymore.

So I'm twenty-one years old, I live in Miami, Florida, and I have no clue what to do with my life. A woman named Barbara Bierman convinces me to start playing beach volleyball. Doubles. Now, no one plays beach volleyball in Miami, Florida, in 1991. It takes a week just to schedule a game. You've got to find two other girls who can get the time off work to drive down from somewhere else.

I've spent my whole volleyball life, short as it is, as a middle blocker, the big one in the middle, the one who touches every ball. I hit and I block, period. That's what the middle blocker does, and I'm good at this, and I only do what I'm good at. I'm still that way; I know what I excel at and those are the only things I go after. In college I was never put in any passing drills, never put in any setting drills, because Cecile, my coach, had wisely figured that she had me for only a short period of time, so she had to develop my strengths.

So I go to the beach. And I have no idea what I'm doing, but I somehow know that this will work out for me. Something I'm very fortunate to possess, more than my looks or even my athletic gifts, is the ability to trust what I know. I grew up trusting myself because I spent a childhood around adults I rarely trusted. At eight or nine, I already had my ideas about what was happening, and I knew I was right. I would confront my mother or other adults, and they would say, "You have no idea what you're talking about; you're too young," and my response would be, "I know what I saw and I know what I think." I developed this capacity very young because I was forced to in order to survive.

In January, shortly after I'd turned twenty-two, Barbara Bierman says, "Hey, we're going to play in this tournament in Puerto Rico for the WPVA, the Women's Professional Volleyball Association. You're going to call the WPVA and you're going to tell them you want to play for them and that they need you." So I do it, and Barbara and I go to Puerto Rico. Our first game is against Jackie Silva, this killer player from Brazil. And we get whacked 15–4, something ugly like that. But still, Barbara says, "California is where all the beach volleyball is. You're young enough and mobile enough and you can do this."

I was in a bad situation. If it wasn't for the help I received from Lily Stefano, a friend at the time, I could not have afforded to move. On my way out to California, broke more or less, I stopped at a tournament in Arizona, where, once again, I was humiliated. That was the week that *People*'s Fifty Most Beautiful People edition came out. There I was, clutching a hot pink volleyball and calling myself a professional volleyball player. Barbara and I played in the tournament and were out–*uno, dos, adios*–but we played well enough. People could see there was some talent there.

So by April I'm living in California with my friend Dan Vrebalovich, and I'm playing doubles and I am dying. Once I had a job in New York and I flew back early to play in a tournament in Santa Cruz. My flight was delayed, I got there an hour late, and even though my game wasn't up yet, they still wouldn't let me play. It wasn't easy.

It didn't help that I was—and am—so hard on myself. Hard on my mother, hard on my partner, hard on just about anyone who's important to me. When you play a sport you never concentrate on what's right. You're always talking about what's wrong with your game. When you do drills, and when you practice, you're always trying to improve, improve, improve. It's never "Hey! I've got that down! Let's do that for a while!"

Over the course of the early summer, I realized that I needed to train and I needed to practice. Badly. I've always had the ability to chart realistic goals. I'm not one of those people who go, "I can't get from A to Z immediately, so I won't even try to go from A to B." I'm a plodder. Training, I realized, was key for me.

In the meantime, I'd become friends with another

doubles player, Holly McPeak. She was almost a rookie, too, and she was really kicking some ass on the tour. People were against her, and I liked her for that, too. She invited me to come train with her and whoever her partner was at the time—doubles is like marriage, divorce, marriage, divorce—and I played with a girl named Lisa Arce. Lisa and I were basically Holly's training victims. We were these big blockers, practice dummies.

I realized I wasn't going to peak that season. I realized I needed to be intelligent: I was not going to win a tournament. I was probably not even going to win a game. So I quit the WPVA. I started training, and I'm practicing and getting a little better, and then one day I get a phone call from a woman named Lisa Strand, who says, "Gabrielle, we're going to do this four-person thing, and would you be interested? We'd like you to be the first pick in the draft." I said sure, even though I didn't know a thing about it. Fours had only been around a year before that, and only guys had played it. One thing I did know: I'd be the one in the middle again.

When a door opens for me I walk right through it. Always. I joined up with Samantha Shaver—now the captain of Team Norelco—and Sherry Boyer, who set for me a little bit last year, and Lisa Strand, and we played in our first tournament and we went 5–0. But the game was different then; we were all indoor girls going, "Well, okay, we'll stumble around and keep the ball off the sand, I guess." If that team was on this year's circuit, we would never have even been able to score.

1(0)

Chicago

IN THE THREE DAYS between Detroit and Chicago, Gabby and coach Gary Sato have renovated Team Nike. Christine "The Rocket" Romero has been let go, and Kim Crawford, another rookie and the former tour alternate, has been drafted in her place.

Team Nike arrives early Thursday afternoon in order to conduct a clinic and exhibition game, part of Nike's PLAY (Participate in the Lives of America's Youth) program. The team is ferried from O'Hare to the site of the clinic in a limousine driven by a Ukrainian emigrant who introduces himself as Leo, lover of volleyball and beautiful American women.

The clinic and exhibition is held at four, at the site of the tournament. The Sony AutoSound truck has just arrived and isn't yet set up to blow out eardrums. The bleachers, still seatless, are a white metal skeleton. Chicago is reputed to be a big beach volleyball city, and North Avenue Beach has a few courts with sagging nets that look as if they get some use. It's a day claustrophobic with clouds, swaddled in dense heat. Someone says the weather report calls for 100 percent humidity.

At the beginning of the clinic there are about a hundred kids. They come mostly from the local Boys & Girls Club, or are the winners of a drawing held earlier in the summer at NikeTown Chicago. They all wear black T-shirts that say PLAY in bright letters, all size X-large. On the smallest children the T-shirts are ankle-length nightshirts. They trip around the court and lurch into impromptu break dances. Nike is donating the volleyballs used at the clinic to Chicago Parks and Recreation, and a few dozen soccer balls as well.

As a favor to Gabby and to round up some good press, Team Discus has agreed to help with the clinic. Gabby and Team Discus captain Stephanie Cox separate the kids into age groups, line them up—easier than it sounds—and begin teaching them the rudiments of the pass, also called the bump.

A female DJ from a local radio show introduces Gabby, making a tired reference to Gabby's height: "I'm usually the tallest girl in the room, but now I'm short by comparison!" This is a common response by the woman who's 5'10" to Gabby's 6'3". It's a novelty for which we run-of-the-mill tall girls are ridiculously grateful: to be around a woman who, for once in our lives, is a whole lot taller.

Then the DJ goes on to say, "Here is a famous volleyball player and one of the most beautiful people in the world—Gabriel Reece!" She mispronounces Gabby's name with a Las Vegas flourish.

On the sidelines are a set of chubby twins age eleven or twelve in overalls with pink spandex sports bras underneath. Their mom is in charge of the enthusiasm. "Do you want to go play with that girl?"

They don't. They'd rather sit on the folding chairs and share a bag of Skittles.

"Come on," says Mom. "She's FAMOUS."

Because the site is still being set up, there is no rock blasting from the speakers; the sound of eight women issuing instructions on passing to a gaggle of kids is a smaller-than-life sound. At this moment, it could be any grade school playground. The lake is oceanic in size, the other side barely visible in the haze. You expect to catch a whiff of salt on the breeze, but it's like laying something on your tongue that you anticipate to be sweet but turns out to be sour. There are willows instead of palms. The air and sand are warm and damp. A bunch of the kids are dancing to the Red Hot Chili Peppers. "I like pleasure with my pain and music is my aeroplane."

Amid the chaos two teams are fielded. At first, the subtleties of dig-set-kill are lost on them. It's get-it-over-the-net whichever way you can. A half-dozen security guards are posted around the perimeters of the court, there for Gabby and Gabby alone, provided by Nike and not by the tour, which is not quite hip to the requirements of their most visible player's fame.

Amazingly, after just one hour of spastic volleying there is something that looks like a game going on. This, of course, is one of the great joys of playing volleyball. In a little over an hour, you can do it. Sort of. There are a million kids on each side, saving them from the difficulty of having to run or dive to get the ball, but there are the three touches, and they've got their high fives down cold. By the end, there are about twenty-five die-hards left.

Afterward, there is a raffle, where there are lots and lots of winners: posters of Gabby, T-shirts, water bottles, backpacks. When Gabby says, "Now we've got some shoes to give away," the kids shriek as though a rock star has just appeared. Then Gabby goes to her post at the Nike booth and signs autographs. Not surprisingly, children are more inclusive, less discriminating than their elders. They want all the players to sign Gabby's poster. Even the woman who works in the Nike booth is invited by one little girl to sign her water bottle. Laird is introduced to the DJ who introduced Gabby. "Are you with the team?" she asks. "I take care of Gabby," he says.

Because Gabby is a Nike athlete and Michael Jordan is a Nike athlete and this is Michael Jordan's town, the Thursday night team dinner is held at Michael Jordan's restaurant. It's Team Discus, Team Nike, Jane, a few NikeTown employees, and me. The fare is down-home, but not so down-home it might scare off tourists. No strange greens that are normally attacked with a Weedwacker, no animals found in a swamp—Juanita's mac and cheese, quesadillas with corn and beans, banana pudding with vanilla wafers. Also a $34 steak, Michael's Pre-Game Meal.

At the meal, I find myself sitting next to Kim Crawford, who hails from central Florida. She looks and behaves like the stereotype of an Iowa farm girl, six feet tall, wavy, wheat-colored hair, blue eyes, old-fashioned manners. She is as nervous and earnest as she is bereft of humor. Tomorrow is her first professional beach volleyball game. After graduating from high school, she went to Finland to play in the European league for eight months, then came home and drove like mad with her mother out to California to enter the draft. That was April. Now, in less than three months, she is on Team Nike.

"This is all happening so fast," she says. "I mean, look, look where I am. Look who I'm playing with." She opens her square, suntanned hand. The palm is smooth and callused, the fingerprints rubbed flat. I think the gesture is meant to take in all the players at the table—Kim is "yes, ma'am" polite, a small-town girl schooled at a Methodist college, a team player (I don't imagine she'd exclude her teammates)—but it's Gabby she's looking at. She is playing with the most famous female volleyball player in the world. That may not mean much to most people, but volleyball is Kim's chosen sport, her life.

I wonder, considering tomorrow's a big day for her, is she apprehensive? She narrows her eyes. "I am nervous. I don't mean for this to sound selfish, but I deserve this. I earned this chance and I deserve it."

Historically, entitlement has never been the question; rather, the issue has been one of opportunity. A scant twenty-five years ago, before Title IX, the landmark act of Congress which mandated that girls have the same chance to participate in high school sports as do their male counterparts, became law, sports for girls was something of an afterthought.

At my average public school in a suburb of Los Angeles, I was on the field hockey team and the volleyball, basketball, and track teams. I swam. I did not play tennis or softball, although there were girls' teams, both varsity and JV. But the boys' teams always had priority if they needed the gym, or a certain diamond for practice or a game, and cramps were still an excuse not to dress out. We held the notion of ourselves as "jocks." But it was a semi-rebellious notion, and there was absolutely no expectation that being a jock would lead to anything beyond a team picture in the yearbook.

Then came Title IX and feminism, and a growing awareness of the benefits of exercise and the explosion of sports as both a legitimate adult pastime as well as a spectator event (Monday Night Football, the harbinger of wall-to-wall TV sports coverage, became a staple of entertainment in 1971). Big girls like Gabrielle Reece and Kim Crawford suddenly had a glimpse of a future where, at least, they could attend college as a student-athlete. Gabby admits that she never would have gone to college had she not been offered an athletic scholarship.

And then, creak, the door opened a little wider, and at last there was a chance of playing *beyond* college. You may have to go to Europe to do it, you may have to have a second job as a receptionist at a chiropractor's office to get by, in much the same way a painter or a musician might, but there were opportunities, however meager. And the girl jocks of the world were into it. And more, their mothers were into it. Their mothers were not saying, as mine did, "But you don't want thighs like a weight lifter, do you?" Their mothers were saying, "Honey! You could have thighs like a weight lifter!" And they were getting in the car and driving their daughters across country on a moment's notice so that they might do something as unlikely as entering the beach volleyball draft. And they were proud of their daughters.

I tell this to Kim, how, when I was in high school—not twenty years ago—my mother was worried that sports would make me too "mannish." I tell her how the girls I knew who excelled at sports were considered as weird as the geeky boys with the plastic pocket protectors who got A's in chemistry. I tell her how the idea that a sport could occupy a place of real importance in a girl's life—not just as a time killer or something that would give you grace and thus charm and thus make you more attractive to boys—was as incomprehensible as finding ice on the moon, and she gives me a look that tells me that sports really are here for girls. Vaguely bored, she looks at me as though I might as well be enthusing about the marvelous invention of indoor plumbing. She is looking at me, as Gabby likes to say, like I'm on glue.

When we come out of the restaurant and are standing on the curb waiting for a cab, a girl comes up with a napkin for Gabby to autograph.

"What we really want is—can my boyfriend show you his tattoo?" she asks. The autograph is actually for the boyfriend. Gabby says why not—this is just the kind of encounter that amuses her. The boyfriend's the one who winds up embarrassed. To show off the fabled tattoo he's got to take off his shirt, with not just Gabby but all of Team Nike and Team Discus and the rest of us standing around on the sidewalk in front of the restaurant, watching. The tattoo is a triangle uniting three smaller triangles that have the words *air, land,* and H_2O printed in the center of them.

"It's uniting the extreme sports, you know?" he asks from the inside of the collar of his polo shirt.

"Sure," says Gabby.

There's always someone who wants you to sign his butt.

FRIDAY DAWNS HOT AND OVERCAST. By ten o'clock it's raining slow fat drops; even the precipitation is too lethargic to really deliver. Like last weekend in Detroit, Team Nike has three games on Friday. The site is still not set up. Teams play while vendors unpack their boxes, and the officials test the time clock. When the players are announced, they don't even bother turning down the tunes. In its sixth year, the tour still seems like an engine trying to turn over on a cold morning. It's a little half-baked, a little minor league–ish. This is also part of its charm. One of the only places to find purity—by which I mean nothing more than genuine *fun*—in professional sports anymore is in sports that haven't quite arrived, where you know for a fact the players are playing for the kick of it and the joy; all you have to do is check out their salary, their playing conditions, and their accommodations—Gabby's room at the Days Inn has no hot water, and both the air-conditioning and TV are broken—to know they are here for love and love alone.

Laird Hamilton, Gabby's man (*boyfriend* is too fey a word to describe their fierce bond), is also here for love and love alone.

In that Gabby can be said to be similar to anyone else, it is someone like Laird Hamilton, who is not simply an athlete, but a pioneer of sorts. Both Gabby and Laird are forging hyphenated careers that have never before existed: athlete-spokesperson-media star-uncompromising individual. Unlike Shaq, the prototype of the entrepreneurial athlete, Gabby and Laird are inventing their sports as they're playing them, weaving the rope at the exact same time they're climbing it.

Although you won't find Hamilton on any formal ten best lists of the world's greatest surfers, he is unofficially acknowledged by "real" surfers and surfing aficionados—people who refuse to turn this most ephemeral of extreme sports into a contest that can be judged—to be the best big-wave rider in the world. To ride the twenty-five- to thirty-foot waves that break once a winter on the outer reef off Hookipa Beach on Maui—waves that Hamilton has been known to launch on without an appreciable rise in his pulse rate—requires more than just gargantuan biceps and the love of the adrenaline dump. You need a board that's short and heavy, one that you can maneuver, that won't fall out from under you when you drop the twenty-five- to thirty-foot drop. You need what Laird and a few of his friends in Maui have invented: the strap surfboard.

More like a snowboard than a surfboard, the board that Laird lives on has thick rubber straps that function in much the same way ski bindings do. To ride the ride this board is built for, you need the assistance of a Wave Runner, or a Jet Ski, to haul you out and get you going fast enough so you can catch the wave as it begins to bulge. Plain old he-man arms won't do the trick in big-wave riding. Can't go fast enough, can't last long enough to get the two dozen rides in a day that you need to perfect the kind of moves Hamilton can do with as much thought as it takes to mow the lawn: 360s and headstands and flips and you name it.

Laird sometimes thinks of himself as a Thomas Edison of the waves; he considers himself an inventor, inventing both the sport and the equipment that goes with it and maybe helping usher in a new attitude in the minds of the people who follow surfing and other extreme sports. The same purists who admire Hamilton's reputation as rebel surfer tend to find the addition of the rubber straps and the Wave Runner a bastardization of the sport.

Like Gabby, Hamilton has an exotic life story, made even more romantic because it was a life in paradise, tinged with difficulty. Born in California, he grew up on rural Kauai, the eldest son of surfing legend and board shaper Bill Hamilton. In those days, Kauai was not yet the island seasoned tourists sought out to escape the sunburned, macadamia nut–eating hordes of Maui; *Jurassic Park* had not yet been filmed there. The Hamiltons were the only white family in their valley, and Laird was the only haole in Kapaa High School. Mothers kept their daughters away from him. He kept to himself. He surfed. He collected so many stitches—more than a thousand, he says—that his father finally threatened to beat him senseless if he didn't stop needing medical treatment.

After leaving high school at sixteen, Hamilton was "discovered" by an Italian fashion magazine and appeared with some regularity in *GQ* before realizing, as did Gabby, that his image had almost nothing to do with his essence. At twenty-two, he found himself under contract with a company that makes sailboard accessories—a deal not unlike Gabby's deal with Nike, albeit less lucrative—in which all he had to do was be Laird Hamilton. In other words, wait for the big waves, then ride them with the aplomb that was already second nature.

Laird has stories that you'd never hear on any urban cocktail circuit. Once he and a friend paddled across the English Channel. He was also an extra in the movie *Waterworld,* which was shot in Hawaii, and while trying to make it back to shore at the end of one day's filming, the Jet Ski he was riding broke down. With night descending, he got caught in the current on the east coast of the big island of Hawaii. The Hawaiian islands are the most isolated archipelago on the planet; you get pulled out to sea here and the next stop is Antarctica. Eight hours later, he was rescued by a helicopter, the useless Jet Ski abandoned. Six months later he got a phone call from a guy in Hilo who happened to be Hawaii's premier Jet Ski mechanic. The ski had washed up on the beach in front of his house; he'd fixed it and wanted to return it to Laird.

This summer with Gabby is the first time in his life he's spent more than a week out of the water, dedicating himself to supporting this woman who has spent her entire life without the support of anyone but herself. He's supportive in a way that a strong woman relishes, nurturing in a way that comes off as chivalrous, not doting and maternal. Between tournaments they train together at the gym—Gabby's trainer, T. R. Goodman, has created a workout specifically for surfing to maximize Laird's already considerable strength and sense of balance—and he accompanies her to volleyball practice in the afternoon. So far, he hasn't missed a single one. His role is varied; he plays on the opposing team (Team Nike, unlike the other women's beach volleyball teams, always plays against men in practice), shags balls, serves for hours on end. In the evenings he sends out for whatever food Gabby's craving or else he makes dinner—big bowls of dark green salads, fat twenty-ounce steaks marinated in salt and not much else, just the way she likes them.

More important—at least as far as the fate of Team Nike—Laird is not simply in the entourage, as the girlfriend of a male professional athlete might be; he is, in effect, a self-appointed assistant coach who is perhaps more invested in the team and the team's happiness and the happiness of the team's captain than is the team's official coach.

"Both Gary and Liane were resentful of Laird's presence," said Gabby after the season was over. "It's easy to blame him for the problems of our team, to Yoko Ono—ize him, but give me a break. What did Laird have to do with the bad decisions I made in the draft? What did Laird have to do with Liane's edginess? What did Laird have to do with Liane's attitude toward Gary, when he would tell her to do something she didn't want to do? The only person Laird affects is me."

In a cover profile for *Outside* magazine, writer Bucky McMahon calls being with Laird "watching an event in progress," so despite Gabby's belief that Laird's presence doesn't have anything to do with the team dynamic, it obviously does. Today, for example, Coach Gary is not here, but at home in California awaiting the birth of his second child. Team Nike is coachless so Laird sits in the players' dugout, doing what he normally does from his spot high in the bleachers—"Communicate, girls!" he roars from the dugout. "Communicate!"

The first match is against Team Discus. With forty-seven seconds left the score is 14–7 Discus. This loss in not unexpected;
after all, it's the first game with Kim Crawford. A new Team
Nike is playing against other teams that have now been together
since the season began. There are few of the rallies, the tap-tap-
tap OVER tap-tap-tap OVER, tap-tap-tap OVER, that gives the
game of volleyball its pleasing rhythm. The game is played in fits
and starts.

The announcer is not their normal guy, but a Chick Hearn
wanna-be who likes the sound of his own voice. The ball has
suddenly become the Mikasa—*the Mee-cah-sah!*—and when the
Mee-cah-sah goes long he yelps, "Hidy ho, neighbor! Peanuts
and cocktails are served on this flight!" Some of the players stare
up at the booth; what is he *talking* about? Several times he con-
fuses the score, then the time.

After the loss, the team sits in a huddle in the dugout, doing a
quick play-by-play, what they did wrong, how they can improve,
what they did right—do more of that! There is a moment during
which Laird is trying to make a point; he leans forward, claps the
back of one hand into the palm of the other, finds first Gabby's
eyes, then Kim's, then Jen's, then Liane's with his own. Liane
turns to the ice chest, rustles through the melting cubes for a bottle of Aqua Fina, stands up, and walks away.

THE SEASON IS ONE-THIRD OVER, and at this point Team
Sony AutoSound looks like the team to beat. There is great parity among the teams this season. This year is unlike other years
on the tour in that all the players are beach players first and fore-

most. Five of the women who usually play on the beach during their off-season are on the U.S. Women's National Team and are busy training for the Olympics. Sony has another big girl in the middle, Stanford's "player of the decade," Kim Oden; Antoinette "Anto" White—who will wind up being this season's offensive player of the year—a slim, quick setter, Chrissy Boehle; and the big and cute rookie, Brita Schwerm. Although they came in dead last in the first tournament in Clearwater, Florida, they came in first in both New York and Detroit. This weekend Sony will go straight to the finals, while Discus and Paul Mitchell will make it into the semifinals. So it's Sony and then whoever's hot that week—Discus or Norelco or Paul Mitchell. So far, Nike has never been hot; they lose their second match to Sony 15–8.

Sitting in the row ahead of me are a trio of brothers, one a half head taller than the next, like Russian nesting dolls. They wear blue and green Hawaiian print trunks—not matching but from the same manufacturer—and their brown backs each display a constellation of angry mosquito bites. There is a little girl sitting next to them, maybe nine years old, permanent teeth coming in making a temporary mess of her smile, her straight dirty-blond hair on a ponytail on top of her head. She folds her arms and lisps, "I'm getting sick of this. I came to see Gabby *win.*"

A game is like a relationship. You enter into it with the highest expectations, never notice the misstep, tiny as a sigh, that sends the whole thing spinning off into doom, then spend an indecent amount of time trying to pinpoint the exact place where things fell apart.

After the game, Gabby comes over and sits down in the bleachers. Her brow is furrowed above her shades. A drop of sweat dangles beneath her chin. People hover around, hoping she'll entertain the idea of some quick autographs, but she ignores them. "In twenty minutes I'll have a different attitude," she says resolutely. She asks if I have any questions for her, anything I have to ask her.

"What happened?" I say.

"You saw it," she says.

"There's never anything to say after a loss," I say.

"Just as many things to say after a loss as a win," she says, "but you don't want to say them."

IT'S 3:00 P.M.; THE CLOUDS have sat swollen overhead all day long. Team Nike versus Team Paul Mitchell, Shoes vs. Hair. Nothing changes weatherwise, and nothing changes Nike-wise. Paul Mitchell racks up three points impossibly fast. "Ka-BOOM!" intones the announcer. "Nobody home at NikeTown!" The first two points are given up by Gabby, her hitting the ball long. It's anxiety, it's frustration, it's rushing. Rushing to get this over with? Rushing to get out of a rut and into a groove? Rushing what, exactly? Then there is a net violation on Nike and the score has suddenly jumped to 5–0.

It's over already, of course. I say "of course" because the day has about it that discomforting predestined, and-so-it-was-written quality, the sense that things have been slated in some unseen realm to go from bad to worse to seemingly unendurable (the lesson in this is always you'd be surprised what you can endure) and no amount of visualizing, attitude readjusting, or strategizing, no energy boost from Power Bars or bananas, no seduction of luck by the application of a lucky shade of nail polish can alter a thing. Even the crowd, such as it is, normally happy just to be sitting there, outside, enjoying the sun, such as IT is, and the music and the babes, is starting to have an opinion. "What gives with this Nike team?" says a guy on a mountain bike from around a slice of pizza.

And you wonder—if people who aren't even paying much attention are wondering this, what's the team thinking? How many demons have found their way into the heads of Jen and Kim and Liane and Gabby and taken up permanent residence? *Maybe we ARE the worst team, maybe we'll NEVER pull this out; what if the entire summer is like this?* Does Gabby ever wonder, *What if I am just a big, pretty girl with some athletic ability but not a real athlete at all?* Gabby knows that whether she plays well or not, it matters to almost no one. To the world she's a supermodel and volleyball player! She's a dog walking on her hind legs. An infamous observation made by eighteenth-century thinker and chauvinist Samuel Johnson about women writers ("A woman's writing is like a dog's walking on his hind legs. It is not done well; but you are surprised to find it done at all") is now applicable to pretty female athletes. It's not that she's gorgeous and plays volleyball well; it's that she's gorgeous and can play it at all.

Later, Gabby will tell me she never thinks like this. *Never.* I don't quite believe her. I think, *They are physically more than capable of doing this. If it's not a head thing, what is it?* Impossibly the score crawls up to 6–0. Nike has NO points. Are they thinking, *What if we never score in this game?* I know I would be. The female tendency to accelerate. *"What if we never score another point* again?!"

It's not as if they're not playing hard. It's not as if Team Nike is just standing there, missing every ball, or hitting it out. In volleyball, terminating the play doesn't earn a point if your side doesn't have service. Unfortunately and ironically, the only time Nike is able to execute is during the side out. Then, once they get the ball back, they can't hold on to it. Back it goes to Paul Mitchell, who racks up a handful of points at a time. There is some diving going on—Liane looks like a sugar cookie rolled in sprinkles—a few heroic saves, but it's not enough, and Gabby starts killing long, and then the jig is up and who even knows what the final score is. It's over, it's over. It's Detroit *all over.*

With 3:23 left on the clock, the score is 4–10. It's ugly. Behind me I hear a guy say, "There's that Gabrielle Reece. She's the tall broad in the middle."

In the end it's Hair, 15–4.

An hour later, I phone Gabby in her room. I'm concerned about her frame of mind, but she shrugs it off, isn't interested in my doting.

"I've won and lost so many times that I don't get overly excited about either one. What I *do* beat myself up about is how I may be failing as a captain. What do I need to do differently? Have I said too much? Too little? Do I expect too much or not enough?"

"It's like being a parent," I say, "no matter what you do, on some level it's not right."

"I take full responsibility when we lose."

"How are the other girls feeling?"

"I don't know. I left. I don't want to create a space for any postgame wallowing. We'd just be saying the same thing we did after we lost the first two games."

"At what point did you think, *Oh, no, this is going to be a replay of last week?*"

"I didn't and I don't. I've been playing long enough to know not to do that. I don't have to tell myself not to do it, I just don't do it. I try to go for long-term thinking. I don't think, *Oh, my God, we lost again!* I think, *Hey, new team, better team, just needs some work.* The problem is, what kind of work? After New York I practiced them hard, Monday, Tuesday, Wednesday, then after Detroit, Monday, Tuesday, Wednesday. The nose-to-the-grindstone thing doesn't seem to be helping, so now I won't call a practice until Tuesday. I don't want to see their faces. We're just not coalescing."

THE TEAM DINNER that night is at L'Angolo di Roma, a few miles away from our hotel, straight up Clark Street. There is a twelve-plate family-style meal that Gabby orders for the table. The tiramisù is brought in a ceramic serving bowl. Throughout the meal, which is a leisurely three hours, Liane and Gabby barely exchange words.

Afterward, Gabby summons cabs for her players—an endearing quirk that might be given to Holly Hunter in a movie—and decides that she, Laird, and I should walk the few miles down Clark Street back to the hotel. The night is sultry, clotted with neon. After a few blocks, Gabby, who got all the food we couldn't finish to go, gives the brown grocery bag of leftovers to a homeless guy who hits us up for change. "This is better," she promises. "I'm telling you, you won't be disappointed."

Even though it's nearly eleven, it's hot time, summer in the city and all that. The streets are crowded with people escaping their stuffy North Shore condos. Gabby's experience of being recognized is a three-part process. The average female celebrity endures a bald stare that evolves into a questioning, reverential gaze: "Is that really . . . *Michelle Pfeiffer?*" The average male basketball player—or, for that matter, any buff-looking guy taller than, say, 6'6"—is hit up for an autograph because he's so big and ergo must play basketball. The first thing someone notices about Gabby is her unusual size—"Wow, she's tall!"—then they peer into her face and it's "Wow, she's beautiful"—the degree of her height plus the degree of her beauty make processing this one a little tough; none of the Jolly Green Giants or Olive Oyls or String Beans from junior high, those monstrous girls who spend their youth wishing they could fold themselves up like a cell phone looked like this—but wait, there's even *more* to this, and it's "Wait, aren't you . . . ?" Few people ever make it to her name. On Clark Street a fourteen-year-old girl roaming with a pack of her friends clamps a sweaty hand on Gabby's forearm, gawks like a talentless actress receiving poor direction to act shocked, and says, "You're . . . you're . . ."

"Hey," says Gabby and keeps walking.

Philosophizing, like wallowing in a loss, is something Gabby does not do. She has developed an uncanny ability to compartmentalize her thoughts, to know exactly how much energy a thought merits. She is the anti-Hamlet. If there is a question that cannot be answered and acted upon, then it's a waste of time asking it. Laird enjoys rumination, however, and as we ramble through the night, we crack open a few subjects normally reserved for after midnight, which is fast approaching anyway.

If playing hard sometimes doesn't guarantee a win and if working hard doesn't work, then what does? If you play hard and lose, then the next time basically just show up and wind up with a win, what have you won? If you put things in perspective—it IS only a game, after all—how do you get jacked enough to win, the purpose of the game in the first place? How *do* you prevent a game from spiraling downward? You see things fall apart, go down down down, and still you're powerless to stop it.

"It's that damn downward spiral," says Gabby. "If I could figure out what to do the second things start going downhill . . ."

We notice suddenly that we're being cruised by a police car. The car passed us once, driving in the same direction as we were walking, turned around in a driveway, and drove past in the opposite direction. Now it was inching past again, slowing traffic behind it. It pulls into a driveway a few feet in front of us and stops, blocking our way. The driver—young, square-faced, dishwater blond bangs matted to his forehead—is wearing a flak jacket. He says, "Gabrielle Reece?"

She stands there and says nothing, as if he might serve her a subpoena or deliver some bad news. I remember her once saying that she is fond of waiting things out, of letting the other guy hang himself, if that's what he's going to do.

"Yeah," says Laird, "what can we do for you?"

"An autograph? And a picture?" The cop goes around to the trunk, opens it, and retrieves an Instamatic from a small blue knapsack. "I always carry this. A lot of famous people come to Chicago. You wouldn't think. But they do."

Laird takes a picture of Gabby and the officer, Gabby and the officer and the partner, Gabby and the officer's car.

THE NEXT AFTERNOON, Saturday afternoon, after a 15–10 loss to Team Norelco, Gabby decides to fly home early. Although she is what most people consider rich, she does not like to spend money. She's not frugal—in her garage at home is a top-of-the-line teal green Land Cruiser—but she buys only what she needs. Money mostly affords her freedom and mobility. In this case, she needs to get home, and since she travels first class (bigger seats, fewer celebrity demands), her reservations are easily altered to accommodate last-minute changes. Jen and Liane stay to hang out and watch the men play. With their restricted must-stay-over-a-Saturday-night–type ticket, they have no choice. They eat the cold-cut sandwiches being offered in the Players Tent, drink big paper cups of Bud Light. They throw their sandy, tired feet up on the folding chairs that begin the day in neat lines befitting a Catholic school assembly and wind up in a jumble by the end of the afternoon.

Who shows up to take Gabby and Laird to the airport but

Leo, the Ukrainian limo driver, lover of volleyball and beautiful women. Before Gabby appears he paces the lobby, worrying that she might take offense at his attire. "It's Saturday. I wore sports shirt instead of suit. She won't be offend, do you think?"

Before Gabby's even settled in the backseat of the car she laces her long fingers over one knee and announces: "Okay. Now the challenge is to get over this, move through this, get on with it. You don't want to get in a rut about something like this." "This," of course, is the losses that have piled up, the bad days and bad matches that have turned, after today, into a full-blown losing streak.

I say maybe some wallowing wouldn't be such a bad idea. Maybe you've got to hit bottom and roll around for a while before you can pick yourself up.

Gabby gives me one of her arctic looks. *Are you on glue?*

Maybe I don't know what I'm talking about. It's one-third through the season and I'm starting to have opinions. I'm an armchair middle blocker: There is the lack of chemistry, the lack of parity. There is Gabby alone with her magnificent boyfriend in her limo with her besotted Ukrainian driver, while her teammates, all without partners and certainly without limos, hang around after the match in their uniforms (unlike almost any other sport, they can go from court to beach without having to change and fit in quite well), drinking beer and eating submarine sandwiches and kibbitzing about their loss. But in any case, they are together. Gabby is singular, her blessing and her curse.

Leo passes a folded newspaper back through the window while he drives. Gabby's interview in the *Tribune*. The headline, and the gist of the article, was that Gabby was doing a lot for her sport. "Yeah, I'm really doing a lot for my sport—driving to the airport while the other teams are still playing."

Laird reads over her shoulder and snorts, "They say you're famous more for your beauty than for your game. Where do they get off saying that?"

"No," she says, "*I* said that."

Laird says nothing, squeezes her hand.

11

Big Questions

I SAID TO A BOYFRIEND ONCE that I believe
there is good and evil in life, real good and real evil. I
believe it's sort of like a game, with each side getting
players for their team. I think that people in positions
of power may be aided by a lot of evil.

My boyfriend believed what most people like to believe, that people are intrinsically good. I believe in
goodness, but I also believe in other things that are
right here with us. And I'm not talking evil sort of
floating around like high clouds, but that major politi-
cal figures are holding hands with Satan—that kind of
evil.

There is a man in my life who helped take care of
me from the time I was seven. Peter Richardson.
When we met, he was seventeen and I was seven. Al-

though he was still in high school, he was taking a college biology class my mother was also taking. One day my mother brought me to class and that's when we met. Peter more or less oversaw my spiritual development. The core of my beliefs and ethics existed before Peter, but his presence in my life brought them to the surface.

But I always thought that Peter was waiting for me. He waited. For years and years. My struggle was that while I loved and love Peter, while I respected him always, I wasn't him. He was so pure and straight and strong. By the time he was twenty-one and I was eleven, we were friends. My mother trusted him implicitly. We lived down in that ravine and he used to come and pick up me and my friends and take us to the beach. He was like my big brother, but I also sensed that he felt something else. And at that time I was very wild. Not wild like makeup and hair, but I was doing my thing.

Peter had a girlfriend, Patissa. And Patissa had a problem with her mother. We knew Patissa and her mother very well. We let Patissa live with us. I am now fourteen. Patissa is twenty. Peter is twenty-four. And Patissa has made up her mind. She is going to get him. She is going to land this boat. And women before had tried. Peter was an incredible catch. Smart, relatively attractive, very interesting, and solid. He was always testing Patissa, who had known him for a long time, and I could see this. I would hang out in her room, lying on her bed with my feet propped up on her wall, and I would say, "Why do you let him do this to you? Just cut the shit, lay it out there." But I could have done that with Peter because I had that kind of relationship with him. It was because of the way our minds both worked.

So I started helping Patissa. I wrote down things she should say—this you say to this, this you say to that. Cyrano stuff. Peter started thinking, *Maybe Patissa gets it. Maybe she is the one.* Peter was devoted to God and could not have a mate who would hinder him. And he and Patissa became very close, but one day she said to him, "You're waiting for Gabrielle, aren't you?" No one had ever said it aloud before. Peter freaked out. Only a few nights before, he had had a dream about me, and when he woke up in the morning he had a long blond hair in his mouth.

But nothing happens between us. I'm fourteen years old, or maybe fifteen by this time, and I'm not ready for him. I'm not ready to admit I believe in God one way or the other. One day, I'm over at his house and he says, "Okay, Gabrielle, you think you're pretty smart, don't you?" And I said, "Yeah," and he said, "I want you to close your eyes and, using only your imagination, create a new color. You can't mix any colors that already exist to create this new color." So I tried this for about one minute and of course it's impossible. Then he says, "Too difficult? Let's try something easier. Close your eyes and, without borrowing from any animal that already exists, create a new animal, an animal that no one's ever seen before. Can't do that either. Because our imaginations don't run that deep. The human imagination can only really derive something; it can't truly create it. But there is one mind that can create on that level—even if you believe in evolution, someone got that ball rolling—and wouldn't you be interested in knowing the mind that would be able to do that?" And that was the day I thought, *That makes sense to me. If you want to talk about religion, I can talk about that.*

So by sixteen I had established a kind of faith that things made sense. I had faith that things were how they were for a reason. I was in this situation with my mother for a reason. I was tall like I was for a reason. As I got older I saw that if you can't find meaning in your life, you can't do what you consider to be impossible. I conduct myself according to what I believe to be a law. Be truthful, work hard, don't hate people—all those fundamentals you learned as a small child. It sounds boring—this moral checklist—but everyone's got to have one. This has helped me tremendously, having a sense of ethics. I won't work with someone I know to be dishonest. I try hard not to lie. And as much as I dislike it, I'm willing to get into a confrontation with someone rather than glossing over what I know to be untrue or not right. My success stems in the end from this.

SO PETER WAS AN enormous influence in my life. But what he had to offer was very contrary to who I was. Here I am, a teenage girl, attractive, very mobile, everything was very accessible to me. But all the while my brain is working, and I'm having all these spiritual conflicts, and I'm rebellious to boot. Even then I was fighting for control. For me to admit there was a higher being was the same as admitting I had no control, and that was a very big deal. What was my God at that time? Getting control. Because for my entire life I'd had no control. Because I'm an up-front, nonhypocritical person, admitting a belief in God would mean trying to live my life according to God's rules.

I decided to be celibate, and I was for two years, from eighteen to twenty. I wanted to see what this God business was all about. And this didn't mean I was going to give up my outspokenness, and I wasn't going to start wearing pink dresses to church. Everyone whom I knew in Florida all had clear skin and bows in their hair, but nobody would say what they thought– they would think it, but they wouldn't say it, and for me that was bad. I was still very harsh, but I wasn't drinking and I wasn't sleeping with my boyfriend, and I was trying to control my thoughts and my negativity . . . if I had an issue with someone I would try to go to speak with them. It was *heavy*.

At this point I started modeling–so there it was, the control I sought. Boom, I was suddenly making my own money. But now, it's guilt-o-rama. I'm making all this money modeling, and I'm still able to go to school and play volleyball, and things, for the very first time, are good for me, but now I'm thinking, *Is this coming not from good, but from evil? Evil can use anything it wants to seduce you. And here I am, making a shitload of money by what? By making myself an object of desire.*

To do this, to walk this thin line, I had to become very hard. I was no longer living my life; instead I was watching it, judging it. I was emotionally disengaged, but I was doing what I thought was the right thing. This is another reason I kept moving toward sports and away from modeling–it eased that conflict.

When I was twenty-one I went back to St. Thomas

to try to put some kind of closure on my life there. I wasn't sure what exactly I was going to do there. I rented a car. I thought I might go by my old house to see that it was just a house and that all the pain I was holding for that place didn't exist. It was just four walls and a roof. I went and saw Peter while I was there. We sat on a dock and had a long conversation.

I told him, almost like a confession, that I didn't do things the way he did, that I didn't think like he did, and that I had to accept the person I was, both the good and the bad. That if I didn't, I'd never amount to anything. I saw Peter briefly one last time when I was twenty-two years old.

Peter was put in my life for a very specific reason, and for me not to own that would be the worst thing I could do. One of the things he encouraged in me was the ability to respect my life. I take care of my body because I understand that it's been given to me; it's not just mine to do whatever the hell I want with it. I know I can have a positive influence in the culture at large, but it's got to be subtle, because that's who I am. There are a lot of athletes who come out and say, "What I do, I do for God. This game, it was for God. This award, it was for God, too." That's their way, but it's not mine.

Once I did confess to a journalist that I believed in

God, but the picture that accompanied the interview was too provocative for one group and the letters started coming: "We looked up to you, and now you've gone and done this. . . ." For me it's not a problem. Hey, I check in with who I check in with and I don't need you to monitor me.

12

The Saints

IT'S SATURDAY NIGHT and we are sitting in yet another groovy Italian restaurant—Lombardo's in St. Louis, Missouri—ordering the hot calamari appetizer and the garlic bread, the chicken marsala and the chicken cacciatore. By the end of the summer, these restaurants will all blend together, as do airports in far-flung cities, and we'll forget where it was that we had the great spinach tortellini and the voluptuous, artery-clogging tiramisù.

At one table, there is Laird, Gabby, Kim Crawford, and me; at another, Jen Meredith, Liane, Gary Sato, and, as Gabby still calls them out of respect and schoolgirl habit, Mr. and Mrs. Sato, who've come all the way to St. Louis, in the life-sucking heat of midsummer to watch their daughter and their son, Eric, play, and their other son, Gary, coach.

Gabby, Laird, and Kim Crawford are eating twenty-four-ounce steaks, which took the kitchen nearly forty-five minutes to rustle up and cook. One of the tournament announcers stops by to give Gabby's shoulder a squeeze on his way out.

Gabby says, "How you doing?" She asks about the announcer's wife.

"We're brawling," he says. "She hates all this traveling. We fight before I leave, then we fight on the phone after I get where I'm going."

"She picks fights so she can be sure that you care," says Gabby. "She wants the intensity of the connection. Call her and tell her you love her. You do love her, don't you?"

"Yeah," he stammers, "of course."

"Just call and say you love her and you miss her, but don't get into a conversation. Pray you get the answering machine."

After he leaves, Gabby leans forward and says, "Did you see how he patted my arm? I've started getting phone calls from the captains of other teams. 'Is there anything I can do to help?' Yeah, I say, maybe I'll resign from Team Nike and reenter the draft and you can draft me."

Imperceptibly, as the weeks have passed and Team Nike has failed to show any signs of life despite roster changes, the roadies, the coaches, and the players for both the men's and women's teams have begun treating Gabby as if she were battling an incurable disease. After yet another loss, no one says much, no words left to say, but they simply extend a hand, a cross between a high five and a handshake, a gentle slap of fingers that says "We're also beyond knowing what's wrong, but we're pulling for you." It's a my-heart-goes-out-to-ya high five; call it a sideways 2½.

This weekend—the word *mercifully* comes to mind—Team Nike is not in last place. On Friday they beat Team Discus (the champions last week in Detroit) in a 16–14 grovel-a-thon and on Saturday they beat Sony AutoSound. Despite getting abused by Team

Norelco 6–15, they are headed for the semifinals for the first time since New York.

The tournament is not being held on the banks of the Mississippi, as you might imagine, but at Union Station, a 103-year-old train station reconceived as a mall/entertainment complex, located a stone's throw from the St. Louis courthouse where the Dred Scott decision was handed down. A brass plaque inside the mall (a stone's throw away from the Sweet Factory and The Body Shop) reveals that the station, built in 1894, is a national historic landmark and was at one time the largest and busiest railroad terminal in the world. It closed to rail traffic in 1978. Now a small man-made lake hugs the mall, the surface broken by the green golfball-sized heads of turtles dog-paddling around in circles. There is a Hooters inside ("Delightfully Tacky, Yet Unrefined!") and a candy store that features, as part of the buying experience, an hourly song-and-dance production where the employees carry on about their locally famous fudge. Beside the lake, separated by a winding pathway, is the train shed, partially enclosed by a high, arching roof of steel beams that cast striped shadows on the lumpy sand that has been trucked in and dumped directly on the asphalt. Parking lot–cum–beach volleyball court.

On Sunday morning, around 8:30, Team Nike and Team Norelco take the court to warm up. In the sunny stripes between the iron beams the sun feels strong enough to induce radiation burns, and as the sun moves, the people in the considerable crowd—this is the hometown of Anheuser-Busch, the makers of Bud Light, the real star of the tour—shift from bench to bench, from folding chair to folding chair, in search of shade.

Gabby and Kim Crawford stand a few feet from each other on one side of the court, each in black running tights and forest-green sports top, practicing passing. Kim is still a little awestruck over her change of fortune, something Gabby is beginning to find worrisome. Yesterday, Gabby asked Kim if, on her way back from the Players Tent, she would fetch her some sunglasses from her duffel bag. Kim returned with two pairs of expensive Oakley shades, unsure which pair Gabby meant. Gabby chose one, then told Kim she could keep the other pair.

"Really?" asked Kim, not used to being given things, much less—as is the case with Gabby—given more of something than she'd ever possibly use. After appearing in a commercial for Coppertone, Gabby was given dozens of cases of sunscreen, so many that she keeps a stack of her favorite sunblock, Shade SPF 30, on a table near her front door and gives them away as hostess gifts.

"Get *over* it, Crawford," said Gabby, smiling but not joking.

Later, Gabby tells Laird, "She can't always be, 'Cool! I got a kill!' She's got to accept all of this—the wins and the losses and the free sunglasses—as part of the game. She's got to be a woman with a mission."

Laird says Gabby should try to give Kim a break. "The newness of all this will soon be gone for her, and then it will be gone forever," he says.

Gabby says nothing, but she's right. Now, while they are warming up, a few minutes before the semifinals are scheduled to start, and Gabby and Kim are passing the ball back and forth—neither of their strong suits, it should be noted—Kim hits the ball out, and one of the ball shaggers, a tall, slow-moving girl from the St. Louis Volleyball Club who can't keep her eyes off Gabby, trudges to the ball and lobs it up and back in. The rest of the players from both teams have finished warming up and are in their respective dugouts smearing on sunscreen or adjusting their visors. The time clock shows less than a minute left. Gabby has turned to face the ball shagger, her back to Kim, and Kim takes this as a dismissal. She's on her way off the sand when Gabby receives the ball from the shagger and treats it like a pass in a game, bumping it over her shoulder to Kim—who is startled. Who then thrusts out an arm and unexpectedly keeps the ball in play. Kim beams; she wasn't expecting it, and is proud of herself for having risen to the occasion. Gabby doesn't say anything; she walks off the court as if Kim didn't exist.

Sitting beside me in the first row of folding chairs beside the court is a father who's brought his eleven-year-old daughter and her friend. Both have braces, Guatemalan friendship bracelets, and bony knees, where all the complicated inside parts can be seen from the outside. They've already grabbed Gabby; their programs are signed, their water bottles, too. The father, who doesn't look like a stranger to either chewing tobacco or harder work than most of us can imagine, sits on the edge of his chair, a sunburned hand cupped around a bright pink plastic camera. When Nike is down by four, the father leans over to me and says in a syrup-thick accent, "Can they win?"

"Yes," I say, "they can. But unfortunately it doesn't mean they will."

"The reason I'm asking is, we drove almost 300 miles—all the way from Kansas—to see Gabby play. We're only here for the morning just to see this match. She's my daughter's hero, Gabby is. She watches her on that MTV."

The daughter nods mutely without taking her eyes from the court. I realize I'm witnessing an event that might one day show up in a Nike commercial. Millions of fathers have taken their sons to see a beloved ball team; thousands of dads have done the same for tomboyish daughters—my own dad indulged my passion for the Dodgers when I was thirteen and took me to a half-dozen games that year—but how many fathers will drive down the block to take their girls to see a female athlete play, much less three hundred miles?

I had one question. How did they know Gabby would be playing this morning? When Gabby is profiled by a local television station, the segment always taped only a few yards off the court, just minutes after a game, before Gabby has had a chance to do much more than towel off, wisps of hair sticking to the sweaty sides of her face, sand caked on parts of her arms and midriff, beautiful but hardly glamorous, they never report the score. They never give any details of the game. It's not sports, it's human interest. How had word reached this doting father three hundred miles away in rural Kansas that Team Nike would be playing in the semifinals this morning? Satellite dish? Internet? Someone down at the local feed store?

The father laughed. "It's Gabrielle Reece," he said, interrupting himself midsentence to snap a picture with the pink camera. In his mind, that explained everything.

There is a moment near the end of the game—another game Nike will lose; it's pointless to recount the name of their opponents or the score, information we traditionally hoard to make sense of a game—when the ball is sent over the net to Nike, an almost lazy, high school girl's volley, something you can imagine getting in there and digging yourself. It will fall in a spot between Gabby in the middle and Kim on the left. There is time after the ball begins its dozy descent, and Gabby just stands there and Kim just stands there and it is clear in that second that this game is already lost, and Gabby is allowing Kim some much-needed on-the-job training, a chance to step up and call it—*me-me-me-ME*—which Kim does eventually, but there is a beat during which Kim hesitates, waiting for Gabby to step in and take charge, and when Gabby doesn't, Kim is forced to dive for the ball. She manages an up—the white leather ball resounds with a smack where she makes contact with the flat of her inner arm—but Gabby is not pleased. A girl less green would have been all over that ball. Later, Kim says, "I thought Gabby had it. She saves our butts a lot. It shouldn't be that way, I know, *I know* . . ." she hits the side of her head with her fist, ". . . but it is. At least for now."

TO REACH UNION STATION MALL FROM the court, it's necessary to pass Vendor Row. Every tournament site is set up differently. Sometimes the booths hawking razors and hair goop and car tunes and T-shirts and suntan lotion are spread out along the ends of the court; sometimes they're huddled in a clump on one end. In St. Louis, they are neatly arranged in two rows; to leave the court means running the gauntlet. St. Louis is giveaway city. Nowhere on the tour is the battle between the sport and its sponsors so evident, Athletes vs. Merchandise. As I emerge from Vendor Row I have accumulated a Bud Light CD case for the car, a packet of Paul Mitchell Super Sculpt and a packet of Detangler, a blow-up beach ball from the *St. Louis Dispatch,* a white plastic visor from Norelco, a small white rubber Mikasa volleyball (suitable for a dog toy), and, a staple of every tour stop, a glossy Sony AutoSound "passport" with coupons for expensive stereo and car alarm systems tucked inside. Employees of Anheuser-Busch patrol the front of the bleachers tossing "bones"–long thin plastic beer glasses that say "Bud Light"–into the crowd. Earlier in the weekend Gabby fielded several eye-rolling requests from half-drunk fans–"Hey, Gabby, sign my bone, would ya?"

Both players and fans of four-person beach volleyball pine for the Bud Light Pro Beach Volleyball Tour to adopt the more traditional (read "legitimate") franchise system enjoyed by hyped-to-the-hilt male professional sports, but it is unlikely to happen anytime soon. Legitimacy in this case has nothing to do with the commitment, perseverance, and dedication of the athletes. Were that the sole measure of legitimacy in professional sports the sacrifices made by most of the women playing on the tour–women who work at other jobs to help support themselves, who live in more humble digs than they otherwise might in order to save money to dedicate their summers to their sport–would make them more legitimate athletes than, say, the male basketball players who have been courted since eighth grade and, as college sophomores, are being lured into the pros with tacit offers of multimillion-dollar contracts.

Legitimacy in sports in the late twentieth century is a matter of aesthetics. If you are a Bear or a Bull or a Cardinal, you are somehow seen as being part of a classier operation. Despite the fact that almost every college football bowl game is owned by one corporation or another and every possible surface in every professional sports stadium across the country is decked with corporate logos, the players' uniforms are pristine, unsullied. No Federal Express or Delta Airlines splayed across the butts of football players or baseball players. They are legitimate because they are at least one degree away from being walking, talking billboards (which is what they are in their off-hours, but no matter); on the field, they are something big and fierce, untouched by filthy lucre. The fact that the team is probably owned by some rich guy whose entire existence revolves around making money is irrelevant.

Overheard: a father trying to explain to his daughter the logic behind the name of her favorite team. "Who is Paul Mitchell?" she asks.

"It's styling products," says Dad.

"You mean, like, for your hair?" she says.

"Shampoo. Shampoo and stuff like that."

"It's not a guy?"

"What's not a guy?"

"Paul."

"No, it's a product, honey, shampoo, like I said."

"They're named for shampoo?"

Dad doesn't answer.

But far better to be Hair than No Hair—Team Norelco. The notion of a razor sponsoring a women's team skitters along the border of bad taste. By the end of the tour, the announcer refers to the team as the Nubs. Often, during a time-out, the announcer will launch into a plug for Norelco, read in High Tongue and Cheek (how else to deliver material like this): "Norelco! Designed to shave a woman where a woman shaves!" which inevitably elicits guffaws from anyone who's actually listening.

Once, while I was sitting at a table in the Invited Guests Section with Laird and some of the players on the men's tour, someone hooted, "And where would that be?"

"Designed to shave a woman where a woman *waxes*," hollered Laird.

Samantha Shaver, Team Norelco's captain, is always intro-duced as "the woman born to represent Norelco, Samantha *Shaver*." The fact that she was the league's 1994 Defensive Player of the Year or a former member of the U.S. Women's National Team is rarely mentioned.

The person responsible for the concept of Team Your Product Name Here is Craig Elledge, president of CE Sports, which bills itself as "the nation's leading lifestyle sports marketing firm and producer of nationally televised sports events." Lifestyle sports are fringe sports that no one can make a living at participating in without another source of revenue or a corporate sponsor: snow-boarding, windboarding, in-line skating.

The office of CE Sports is located in Van Nuys, deep in the DMZ of Southern California's San Fernando Valley, a million miles from the beach and everything it stands for. While the close-in valley suburbs of Encino, Sherman Oaks, and Studio City have gained some cachet as Los Angeles has continued to sprawl, Van Nuys is still a depressing conglomeration of wide, straight streets lined with decaying strip malls and tract houses with bars on the windows and dusty Camaros abandoned on weedy front lawns. CE Sports is located on an odd side street that is not industrial, commercial, or residential. The only indica-tion that this isn't an auto detailer or a radiator repair shop is a clunky portable basketball hoop outside the front door.

CE himself is gray-eyed and boyish; he could be a cousin of Michael J. Fox. A graduate of the University of Southern California, the alma mater of both H. R. Haldeman and George Lucas and a major party school, Craig Elledge is not burdened by modesty. He is happy to talk about the success of four-person volleyball, which he takes full credit for inventing.

"I created fours for Anheuser-Busch. Busch is the biggest beer distributor in the country, and they saw the success Miller had with beach volleyball [Miller sponsors the men's Doubles league, the Association of Volleyball Professionals] and they wanted in."

He fondly recounts the creation of the women's tour as if it were itself some mythic homecoming game of yore. In 1992, ESPN came to him in early July and said they had eight hours of programming they needed to fill. On the spur of the moment, he rounded up Liane Sato and Karen Kemner of the U.S. Women's National Team, along with two other players, and dragged them to Irvine to shoot a single match. This, according to CE, was all done more or less intuitively. He twisted arms at Anheuser-Busch and got Bud Light to kick in $10,000. "It was like doing a pilot for TV," he says. "There was no league, no team sponsors, no *teams,* and ESPN saw the pilot and said to me, 'We need women's beach volleyball by August.'

"It was scramble city. I raised $300,000 in three days. All the sponsors we have now we nailed then in that three-day period. It was the same time that Gabby appeared in *People* as one of the fifty most whatever, and she came and said she wanted to play and I said, 'You wanna be a captain? You're a captain!' I had no idea who she was. I drafted her over the phone.

"Sports at this level is just scraping by. We don't have tickets or parking revenue. Even so, we've come farther in six years than baseball did in twenty-five. It's the best idea I've ever had. Why? My main motivation in creating fours was how can I make a game that's a good sponsor vehicle? And the thing is, it's also a great game."

THROUGHOUT THE SUMMER CE shows up at the Southern California venues now and then, but he skips the midwestern stops, except for St. Paul, Minnesota, which is the weekend after St. Louis. The reason he is in St. Paul is history making: For the first time since the league began six years ago the finals are being televised live on a major network. CE Sports has paid for the privilege. A three o'clock Sunday afternoon slot in mid-July that conflicts with no other sports costs $250,000.

CBS has as many semitrailers and trucks on site as the tour itself. They arrive at the Taste of Minnesota on the State Capitol grounds the day before the tournament begins. The court is created on a parking lot adjacent to the fair, which features exhibitions of country line dancing, booths selling tie-dyed T-shirts and incense holders, and a long row of tents offering paper plates bowed with Granny Smith apple slices and caramel for dipping, Sno-Kones, and pork chops on a stick. The players are staying in yet another Ramada Inn fifteen minutes away from downtown St. Paul, graceful in a melancholy way, like a once great middle European capital. The Ramada Inn is stranded in a neighborhood arranged around an off-ramp, with a SuperAmerica mini-mart/gas station and the hotel on one side and a string of fast-food joints on the other. The hotel elevator and lobby reek of that now familiar cheap disinfectant, the smell that reminds you of every bad wedding reception you've ever attended in your life.

Between St. Louis and St. Paul Gabby thought about doing what she termed spring cleaning, getting rid of both gentle Jen Meredith and feisty Liane Sato. "The vibes are just so bad," she tells me over the phone. When I ask her what releasing Liane will do to her already tense relationship with Coach Gary, she says, "He may not want to coach me anymore, but I've got to be prepared for that. I'm bummed, you know? I used to have a real relationship with Gary, a friendship. But now it's de-evolved into this chilly working relationship. He's not the same, somehow. I get frustrated and I think he's just had this healthy, wonderful child, why doesn't he have more perspective on things?"

The moments when I remember that Gabby is only twenty-six years old are infrequent. Most of the time her grace and confidence, her high degree of achievement make her seem ten years older. Laird and I, who both have a few more years on us, say, "It should be enough, the birth of a child, but sometimes it just isn't." She says a little petulantly, "Well, it should be." We agree. We also say that life is more complicated than that.

Every Monday at noon is the deadline for releasing players and picking up new ones. Sundays—days in which she used to regularly play in the semifinals and often finals—are now days when she agonizes. "I was a total wreck," says Gabby of the day she returned home from St. Louis. "Jen left a long message on my answering machine saying she knew she hadn't been playing up to her abilities and she knew she was on the verge of being cut, but please *please* have patience and give her another chance. So even though I was ready to lose both Jen and Liane AND Gary, I decided instead to get into my Total Motivating Mode."

If Gabby were the kind of person to have regrets, this would be something that, several weeks down the road, might qualify.

In St. Paul, Nike has a new stance on the court. They all wear black tights and black sports tops, logoless save for the elegant white swoosh streaking across their chests. Next to the hodgepodge of sports tops, T-shirts, swimsuit bottoms, bicycle shorts, and tank suits worn by the other teams, Nike's uniform registers as evening wear, or the attire of movie bad guys preparing for a break-in. During their service, the three who are not serving stand together at the front of the net in bomber squadron formation, bent down, hands on knees, eyes invisible behind their wraparound shades.

It isn't enough.

During their first game against Team Paul Mitchell, they hop out to an 8–5 lead, but when they side out again Gabby gets frustrated.

"Wake up, Jen!" she shouts. At 11–11, with 2:19 left to play, both Kim and Jen send serves straight into the net. In the end, it's decided by the clock. Hair 13, Shoes 11.

Afterward Gabby sits alone in a folding chair in the shade outside the Players Tent, brooding. While she rarely disappears after a humiliating loss, although the impulse to run and lock herself in the nearest Porta Potti has got to be there, she doesn't disguise her moods either. Wisely, she refuses to bear the burden of false cheer.

"God, did you see me?" she asks. She says nothing about the

other three women dressed in Nike attire who showed up on the sand at the same time, who played, it seemed, according to their own notions.

The Tuesday before, between the disappointment of performing poorly in St. Louis and the ongoing anguish over whether to revamp the team this late in the season, Gabby took the red-eye to New York, where, on Wednesday, she played in a benefit tournament for football great Boomer Esiason's Heroes Foundation, dedicated to finding a cure for cystic fibrosis. After she arrived at the beach with a team she handpicked herself—Jen Meredith, and Stephanie Cox and Katy Eldridge from Team Discus—and professionally pounded a team that consisted of Boomer Esiason, Ronnie Lott, and two other guys, her mother, Terry, showed up. Then, on Thursday morning, Gabby flew back across the country to Los Angeles, where, on Friday morning, she caught a flight to St. Paul.

I sit beside her; we stare straight ahead. I say, "You are too hard on yourself." I mention the chronic, low-grade stress of the mounting disaster that the season is becoming (I don't frame it in those words, although Gabby wouldn't have minded; she has no use for euphemism), the pressure to make overnight decisions regarding roster changes, the travel, the energy drain of celebrityhood, the nature of her relationship with Terry, and she gives me the arctic freeze. *And your point would be?*

But there are still more matches to be played, which is the thing of it always in sports. However bad it is, there is always a chance of redemption. Later in the afternoon, without any kind of meteorological fanfare, the dead yellow sky turned dead gray. It's now ninety degrees and threatening rain. In round four,

Nike's second game of the day, they pull out a win against Team Sony AutoSound, 15–12. These wins don't look effortless. Every kill, every up, every side out is a close call, a reason for hanging out the flags, declaring a federal holiday. Near the end of the match, the side out goes back and forth six times. It can't go on like this, eking out wins. It starts to rain, those bloated drops that are the hallmark of summer rain here. The CBS lackey in charge of mounting and caring for the TV camera on a platform at one end of the court hurriedly swaddles it in several garbage bags nabbed from empty cans.

At three-thirty, with two matches left, a thunderstorm arrives. The sky above St. Paul's majestic capitol dome is bisected by a crack of lightning. People who've brought umbrellas to shade themselves from the sun are ready for the rain; nonetheless, they hastily clear the stands. In a matter of minutes the sand turns from dark beige to gritty brown mud. We wait. By four-thirty the day has turned dark. Beneath the several inches of trucked-in sand is an expanse of black asphalt. The water can't be absorbed the way it would on the beach, and within minutes pools of brown muck form on the court. Soon a river flows between the court and the curb, where a row of seats are set up on a strip of grass. Players, roadies, and spectators huddle beneath the tents, waiting out the downpour.

I run into CE having a snack in the Invited Guests Section. The catering here is curious. In the great, sopping heat, there is an impressive array of hot, greasy food, the kind that would ap-peal after a day spent snowshoeing–potato cubes sautéed with red peppers and beef rolls that look to be part of the Alpo food group. CE is nibbling on a dinner roll.

"There's either team chemistry or there isn't," he says by way of greeting.

"Is that what's going on, do you think?" I ask.

I wonder where the chemistry is lacking exactly. There are other teams in the league who won't be taking a vacation house together anytime soon, and yet they're still going to the finals and winning the occasional tournament. What is it exactly with Team Nike?

"To tell you the truth, Gabby has drafted poorly the past few years. We've sat in that room during the draft and watched her and our jaws have dropped onto the table. What is she doing? Liane Sato?"

I said I could see the potential conflict. Liane, the Olympic medal winner, the only daughter in the Sato volleyball dynasty, and, even more problematic, a onetime captain herself, who gave up her captainship of Team Paul Mitchell to play for Gabby . . .

CE puts down his roll and taps the crumbs from his fingertips. "She was asked to give it up. Didn't like her style. There were the rumors, too. That some of the girls refused to play for her."

"She's such a strong player, though. And experienced . . ."

CE shrugs. "Like I said, that's why this is such a great game."

It rains hard for just over an hour. One of the tour roadies goes from the Players Tent back to the Invited Guests Section and back again, tugging at the sides, making sure water doesn't accumulate in pockets on the slanting roof. The air smells of damp plastic. Laird, Coach Gary, and two of the other coaches go out on the court and play a game of doubles. They shake their hair like big dogs. Talk circulates that the final two matches of the day—one of which is Team Nike versus Team Norelco—will be postponed until 7:00 A.M. the next morning. Eventually the rain passes, however, and the tournament resumes, hours behind schedule. The wet sand is packed and heavy. Dry dirt has some give. In these conditions, the players leap for a ball and topple over like trees. Nike loses 4–15.

That night, on the way to yet another Italian restaurant, wedged in the center of the backseat of a compact rental car we've dubbed The Clown Car for its miraculous ability to contain a half-dozen very large people, Gabby cries. Nobody says anything. Laird, surfer of the world's biggest waves, is intrepid; you'd have to be to step in now. He finally says, "Maybe you need to think about asking the Lord for help."

"Lover, don't you think I've already tried that?" she says.

13

The Man/Woman Thing

I CAME TO BELIEVE at a young age that guys should be complemented as much as girls on aspects of their sexuality. Men should know if they have incredible physiques, if parts of their bodies are exceptionally beautiful. You've got to let them know what's good about them so they can work it. A woman's looks are scrutinized and commented upon as a matter of course, and it should be the same for men. I had one boyfriend, I told him he had beautiful private parts and he was shocked—that I observed this, then came out with it. I told him it had nothing to do with love—although I did love him—but was simply a fact.

Despite the trend to view the sexes as more alike than not, men and women view sex very differently. Always have, always will. For young girls, it's about getting love. To feel beautiful and cute and desirable. Boys are horny; they just want to get off. But women are much more attached to sex because they're trying to get something out of the relationship that they're not able to get through asking for it, or demanding it, or requiring it—whatever you want to call it.

It's a mistake. Using sex as a tool is a sure way for a woman to fail to command respect. Using sex as a weapon is the worst thing a woman can do, because then she's taking something that's very pure and beautiful and corrupting it; ultimately, she'll pay for it.

The crude term "getting a piece" is accurate for men and women. When you become intimate with someone, you are giving a part of yourself away. So if you look at someone you don't respect, you don't really even like, and you're giving them one of the most sacred things about yourself, you're spending yourself on something that isn't worth it.

Still, I've always had a very hard attitude about sex. A lot of female athletes do. At a young age I saw that contrary to the conventional wisdom, there's no real power in sex. Even for a beautiful girl. You won't get the things you think you'll get from it. If communication and love and trust and respect and friendship haven't been established in a relationship, sex isn't going to achieve it either. It's easy for it to become simply another physical act, no different than picking up a ball and throwing it.

In addition, sex makes women weak. It's a thing that, once a girl gives it up, she gives up her strength. So I used to be really nonchalant. With guys I'd let them know, "Hey, it was *nothing* to me." That's why I went celibate—I realized what a terrible attitude I had. I was protecting myself. I wasn't going to be taken advantage of. Of course, that's why guys act nonchalant. If they're conscious that they're making love to a woman and not simply fucking her, they've given up more than a woman has. It's a much farther road for a guy to travel.

People say someone like me can have any guy I want and that's why I can be so cavalier. But what's the point? I've seen a number of beautiful women play with sex that way. In modeling, perfect example, I can tell you ten girls who can get any guy they want for real. But it's the wrong idea. To bag someone is not difficult. Shit, any regular girl who wants to go sleep with Joe Superstar Athlete can get a game schedule, put on a short dress, and go hang out at the arena the night his team's in town, and she's got a pretty good shot of getting some action. The only thing that separates me from that girl is that I have access to a number of different kinds of people, but getting some guy is no more an accomplishment for me than it is for her.

In the past in my relationships with men, they're immediately impressed with my looks and my athleticism, but once they get to know me they're like, "Ho, okay." They don't expect that the most powerful thing about me will turn out not to be my legs, but my mind. Because I've spent a great deal more time developing my mind than I have on my body, and as far as my looks go—an accident of birth, I don't have anything to do with them.

My physical beauty is dull compared with how I think and feel, but I almost never get to talk to anyone about those things because so few people are interested or able to provoke that kind of response in me. It's very private. I'm not going to give just anyone access to what really fuels me. In interviews sometimes I'll be very straight and heavy—nonperky and not particularly quotable—and the interviewer's eyes will glaze over. He doesn't want to touch it because it's out of the guidelines. People are already pissed off at me because I'm athletic *and* beautiful; to be smart in addition to that . . . it's, like, too much. It's "You're breaking the rules already, Gabrielle—that's okay, we'll let you, but there ARE limits." I've learned not to let it bother me.

Every individual has to stay true to his or her thoughts and beliefs. Got to.

You've got to know what the hell you think and feel because if you're going to ask for it, if you're to *demand* it, you better know what it is. That's one of the things about sports—it provides an arena to practice on yourself. It's so easy to complicate your life with a million energy-draining *issues*. If you play sports, the issues resolve themselves. Self-esteem, self-confidence, your relationship with your own body—a lot of women spend a lifetime bogged down dealing with this stuff, when frankly there are a lot bigger and deeper and more interesting things in life that need to be dealt with. Most women are not going to be in sports forever, so while you're young it's good to dig in, wrestle with all those basic questions of self. That frees you then to start chipping away at the larger questions. I'm not suggesting that learning self-confidence or self-esteem doesn't take some work, but there are more important questions—Who am I accountable to? What is God? Why are we even here?—answering those questions for yourself takes considerably more work. And the answers do not benefit you the woman or you the athlete or you the successful businessperson or you the model; it's for your soul.

The trick is not finding someone to love you, but

finding someone to love, someone you respect. I really wanted to find someone I could admire. I don't mean as a physical specimen, I mean the way he acts toward other people, the way he thinks, his personal mission in life. It's been very hard for me to do because I demand and require so much of myself. And I've got to be able to see it—that's something else. For me he's got to have this raw, primitive, animalistic but yet intelligent and intellectual thing all wrapped together, and that is a very difficult thing. I want someone who's very spiritual and thoughtful and deep and, by the way, can you also be George of the jungle? I'm skeptical of the guy who drives too nice a car and wears too many nice suits. Something in my intellect will say, "If that's important to him, then what else is important to him that's not important to me?"

I'm not a flirtatious woman. I don't use my sexuality that way. Because it's so real for me, I don't flirt unless there's a reason. I don't play games and I'm not a very telling person; I flirt knowing that the next thing is the next step. It's flirting as communication.

But when I met Laird, his effect on me was remarkable. I'm a very hard person, very realistic, but my attraction to him was immediate. I was in Hawaii to film seven segments of *The Extremists* in seven days. Every sport got one day. I'd spent only one afternoon with him doing strap surfing, and we were standing in the parking lot at the beach at Hookipa. I walked over to say good-bye. I was in my bathing suit, with a towel on, and he was soaking wet, and I remember it perfectly. It was the weirdest sensation. I'm so professional. When I work with people I'm very cool, and I make it fun and easy, but there are definite parameters. Being open and easy and warm is part of the professionalism, it's creating the right environment so the show can happen. I gave him a friendly hug, sort of stiff, and caught sight of his hair in my peripheral vision, and I remember not knowing what to think. This is amazing for me; I always know what to think. I had the most terrible feeling, driving away, that I would never see this man again.

I was back in California, at home, and I was *miserable*. You've got to understand how unlikely this was for me. I've never been this way about a man, even in high school. This is how pathetic I was: I had a tape of surfers that showed a clip of each guy riding. I remember eating lunch with Janie, and I put the shot of Laird on pause and said, "Can we just eat lunch with Laird? Please?" She's never seen me this way. Normally I call the shots, normally it's "this is the way it is; if you don't like it, get out." And then I had to go to New York to go to some meetings, and I was supposed to have lunch with JFK, Jr., to talk about writing for *George,* and at the last minute I changed restaurants and he never got the message, and I thought, *If you get the message, baby, great, but I'm not chasing you, there's only one man I'm chasing and he's a surfer who lives in Hawaii.*

My aunts and uncles freaked about Laird. They've always seen me in complete control, and with Laird it's pretty balanced. There's also the fact that Laird has such a profound relationship with the ocean; I think they were thinking that here was a repeat of my dad and my mom. My dad was from the islands; he was very much a free spirit. *Here we go again,* they were thinking, *two very beautiful people, two very* tall *people.* They've always been very warm to all the guys I've brought around, but they didn't know about Laird.

I'd like to believe that Laird and I were each other's destiny, but the problem with that is that he was married once already, and he had a daughter with his then wife, and so it's hard not to think that maybe *she* was his destiny, but he believes that he had to have a relationship with her and go through what he did with her to prepare him for someone like me. Fate is always double-edged.

But Laird has been able to accept and appreciate my essential nature . . . which is the hard stuff. But as tough and as strong as I am, that vulnerable side is equally needy. As Laird says, "Bright light, dark shadow." My attitude toward him isn't "Hey, where are you going? Who was that girl you were talking to? I saw you looking at her." I don't care about any of that. I'll never go through his stuff. I'll never tell him not to look at a beautiful woman. My vulnerability is so deep, so profound, that my partner's got to expose himself as much as I do. To Laird I say, "I want your blood." If I reveal myself to someone, then that person becomes accountable to me because I've shown them everything. And they've got to be prepared for this: I push myself every day, whether it be emotionally, physically, or spiritually, so you better be ready. That's just my nature. And Laird accepts this, respects it, and loves it.

It took a man as male, as authentically male, as Laird to allow me to be female. Any other guy I would have stomped all over. In my outer life, in the way I move and talk, I'm so clearly female, but my energy is so masculine. But beyond that, what appeals to people is the strength I project, having nothing to do with maleness or femaleness, and everything to do with all I've been through.

I like sex to be more like a fight than making love. When I'm in a relationship I'm good to the man, and I expect the same from him. We speak to each other with respect, we communicate, we defer to one another. In that way, we're making love all the time. I like sex to be an exploration of another side, a more aggressive side. I think it should have as many tones and moods as the lighter, more visible sides of life.

This is not always easy. I've had one serious relationship where it broke the relationship. My boyfriend said, "If I didn't know who was talking, I would think that you were the man and I was the woman." Because I demand so much respect and nurturing every single day, all day, I don't need it behind closed doors. I'm not one of those women who would suffer in a lousy relationship and then be grateful because I get a little sweetness and affection prior to sex.

14!

Huntington Beach

THE TOUR RETURNS to the West Coast in the middle of the season, the middle of the California summer, smoggy but cool. The Olympics are still several weeks away, and every other magazine cover is featuring female Olympians; more women are slated to participate this year than ever before in the history of the games. The covers of newsmagazines show women with serious snarls, flexed muscles, in their shorts or suits or cleats—look at these jocks!—while the covers of beauty and style magazines give the same basketball players and swimmers and baseball players the female celebrity treatment—makeup artists, hairstylists, air brush*istes*—rendering them safely feminine (and curiously, less overtly sexual) but virtually unrecognizable as the Women We Love Who Also Kick Ass. We give lip service to our acceptance of women as equal parts tough and soft, but our true perception of what it is to be both feminine and physically intimidating is like the washer/dryer, a favorite home appliance of the '60s that failed to get clothes either quite clean or quite dry. Our female

Olympians are considered less important than male Olympians (except female gymnasts, who are more respected for their degree of suffering—very female—than their sportsmanship) and less feminine than the models and actresses and singers, the anchorwomen, authors, and artists, who are put forth as successful women. Less feminine, and therefore less pretty, less seductive, less everything womanly.

But the woman who is at the vanguard of what has been called The New Female Athletic Aesthetic, who represents as well as any woman can the successful integration of all these conflicting attributes, isn't paying much attention to images of women in the media at this moment. Halfway through her season, she is still in the frustrating position of trying to assemble a team that can *place,* much less win.

Gabby talks often about her willingness to "grind." She describes herself as a plodder, as someone who feels the need to work continuously. Because she's an athlete, people assume this means lifting heavier and more weights, running more sprints, holding longer, more grueling practices. But there's also work involved in being willing to have a confrontation rather than being agreeable, rather than glossing things over—never easy for anyone, more difficult for a woman, especially one in the public eye.

Unlike most professional sports where the usual chain of command is owner over general manager over coach, the captain of a beach volleyball team has the power to fire and hire the coach. On Monday night, July 8, Gabby pays a visit to Gary Sato to tell him she is letting him go. For three and a half seasons he has been her coach, and although this is a painful way to end, he admits that it wasn't working and wasn't much fun. The three-day weekends were killer, and even though he was making roughly twice what the other coaches were, he still wasn't happy.

At the same time, she stops in to see Liane, currently staying with her parents, who live in the same apartment complex. Liane isn't home, and after waiting for an hour or so for Liane to show up, Gabby goes home and leaves a message on Liane's machine. Liane returns the call, leaving a message on Gabby's machine. Their inability to communicate remains constant to the end.

But a setter with Liane's strength, quickness, and experience will always be in demand; a day later Kim Oden, captain of Team Sony AutoSound, perturbed with her own team's 0–4 record in St. Paul, released her setter, Chrissie Boehle, and picked up Liane. Gabby knew that Kim O., as she's called on the circuit, was "ready to blow brain" and had put in a courtesy call to Kim before the trading deadline to let her know that Liane would be available. "Kim O. is killer," Gabby will say later. "She wrote me a nice note saying, 'Thanks for your professionalism and candor. Good luck the rest of the season, and with Laird.' Is that amazing or what? Someone like that *deserves* honesty and candor."

The fallout of all this is some backbiting and gossip. Although Gary Sato was not unhappy to be relieved of his duties (nobody relishes getting the ax), in order to do a little face-saving, he phoned Stephanie Cox. He said, "Now that we're no longer competitors, I wanted to tell you how great you're doing this year, and what a great captain you make, unlike some people we know." One quality many professional female athletes seem to have in common is straightforwardness and an intolerance for duplicity, and Stephanie Cox is no exception. She calls Gabby and tells her everything Gary has said, and Gabby, unwilling to let even this kind of low-grade virus get a foothold, drives over to Gary's chiropractic office at 7:00 A.M.—she has to train at 7:30— and waits for him to arrive. She tells him she won't put up with this kind of crap, he is suitably embarrassed, and that, more or less, is the end of it.

THE NEW COACH of Team Nike is Charlie Brand, head of the Orange County Junior Volleyball Club and the Balboa Volleyball Club, coach of the University of California, Irvine, Men's Volleyball Team. With his thinning blond hair, a nose that looks as if it's spent a lifetime sunburned, and big personality, he's what you expect a beach volleyball coach to be like: an aging beach boy.

When Charlie Brand watched the tapes of the old Team Nike, he shook his head. "There is absolutely no synchronicity here," he said. "A team should move as a unit, kind of like if you've seen strands of kelp move in the current, it all moves in the same direction at the same time. It's like that. These guys are . . . I don't know what they've been doing, frankly."

The new, improved Team Nike looks like this: Jen Meredith will move from outside hitter to setter, the position she played in college. Katie Haller, who played for the University of Southern California Trojans and will be beginning medical school there in a matter of weeks, will take Jen's place as outside hitter. Kim Crawford will stay on the outside, and Gabby will, of course, stay in the middle. On their first day of practice together, Kim said, "This is the first time we've had a real practice and not a rag session."

The sand on Huntington's main beach is powdery and pale. A dust cloud springs up whenever a player dives for an up. Even though there's a continuous breeze, the sand is burning by early afternoon, and one by one the players pull on their white socks.

Even though the site is laid out in the same manner at every tournament—the court with its red fabric lines that look like long seat belts, the bright blue plastic folding chairs and patio tables, each one topped with a navy blue and white Bud Light umbrella, the bleachers framing the court, each corner marked by a giant balloon, the white Paul Mitchell shampoo bottle, or the red Outdoor Products knapsack that for weeks I mistook for a heart—here there is a feeling that one high, hard serve could be picked up by the breeze and cast into orbit or tossed over the channel to Catalina Island. The eastern and midwestern sites, with their makeshift beaches in parks and on parking lots, felt confined by comparison.

The crowd consists of friends of the players, old roommates, classmates from college, cousins. They're savvy. They have their teams they root for; most people who root for Team Nike are rooting for the team, not simply for Gabby because she is famous.

Earlier in the season when it became apparent that Team Nike would not handily sweep the league, and then a little later when it became apparent that just landing a berth in the semifinals each weekend would be a struggle, and a little later when the alarming realization sunk in that the team could conceivably spend the entire summer in last place, never able to put together two wins in a row, I started imagining that maybe what needed to change was not team personnel, but location. Maybe they needed to be back on the home coast—home coast, home court, Pacific standard time, the breezy beach, the familiar bed.

Unfortunately, this is not the case. For now, halfway though the season, there's another factor to consider. The other teams have now played together for months; they've become that kelp, waving together in the current. They know one another, one another's moves, one another's strong points and weaknesses. Regardless of whether the new, improved Team Nike is superior to the old, dysfunctional Team Nike, they're now up against something insurmountable: before today's tournament they'd practiced together only twice. They're essentially strangers familiar to each other only because they wear the same uniforms. The normal variation of team sports—sometimes you get the bad calls, sometimes you have an off day, sometimes your opponent is simply on fire—is a liability for this team when playing well, a catastrophe when it isn't.

Nike goes 0–3 on Friday, then loses again on Saturday. The unbearableness has taken on new shadings, a more exquisitely awful variety of salt for the wound. Team Nike and its exes have started to seem like characters in an Updike novel, where couples who were best friends both divorce and remarry the other ex-spouse. When Team Sony AutoSound plays Team Nike, Liane Sato, Sony's new setter, sashays around in a new green and yellow plaid tank suit, SONY AUTOSOUND printed in white letters across the small of her back. She is more focused than she has been all season; she sprints around the court throwing herself in the way of the ball and delivering a half-dozen applaud-inducing ups.

The announcer is also getting into the act. When Nike, playing Team Norelco, the score a humiliating 0–7 with a full eight minutes still left on the clock, puts a point on the board he says, in mock shock, "Point for . . . wait, am I seeing this right . . . Nike?" After Nike's final game of the tournament against Team Paul Mitchell, he says, "So Paul Mitchell's record remains unblemished . . . as does Nike's."

LAIRD, GABBY, AND I DRIVE home in Laird's huge black Ford pickup truck, his banana-yellow surfboard poking out the back. On the way from the court Gabby is as distressed as she ever allows herself to get in public. Normally, her bearing is imposing. She looks people in the eye with a neutral expression on her face, neither embracing them nor rejecting them. Today she stares down at the pavement. She is intercepted by a few guys who ask, for a change, to take both her and Laird's picture. By way of peculiar introduction they say, "You're going to hate us, but we're from Pennsylvania and we don't see things like this very often."

Once in the car, we pull onto Pacific Coast Highway, and Gabby directs Laird to make a beeline for The Chocolate Factory, where we buy enough Thingamabobs—Rice Krispies squares fortified with peanut butter and marshmallows and covered with chocolate—to earn ourselves a free pound of fudge. Back in the car, Gabby disparages Kim, "She's so high-strung!"

and Jen, "Is she ever going to pick up her feet?" She finishes her
Thingamabob, licks her fingers.

Was it uncomfortable seeing Liane? Playing against Liane?

"Now that Liane is playing for someone else she's not my
problem. I don't think about her. What I do think about is, can I
keep doing this? Cutting people? Kim, Jen, Katie, myself. That's
it! I'll cut myself! You know it's got to be bad when other captains are pulling you aside and offering advice. And can you believe Kim's back talk? Did you see where I go, 'You run up and
block whoever,' and she goes, 'I *can't*'? Doesn't she know me
well enough by now? Doesn't she know that I will cut everybody
every single week if I have to?"

After a few minutes, she rests her head on Laird's shoulder,
then falls asleep like children do, oblivious to the discomfort. Her
sun-bleached hair covers her face, her head slips forward, so that
Laird has to place his hand under her cheek to keep her from
falling.

Gabby lives in a tall house of custard-colored stucco, built on a
hillside, with views of the sea from the top floors. She does not
own the house, but rents it from another volleyball player, a
woman who plays doubles. If Gabby's mind could be expressed
as an interior, it would probably look much like the inside of this
house, which manages to be spartan without being monastic,
with large pieces of stressed pine furniture and living room walls
painted a shade of green that would appeal to Matisse. There is
nothing unnecessary here—no knickknacks, few wall decorations
save a bright painting over the fireplace, no old magazines or
coupons or dead pens that seem to clutter up the counters and

coffee tables of other houses. It is organized in a way that is calm-ing, not bereft.

The guest room has a high sleigh bed, a reading lamp on a blue oval bedside table, and a large Sony Trinitron TV; Gabby's bedroom, bathroom, and office are on the upper floor. She gives you the run of the house, shows you where the washing machine is, where the munchies are kept, and how to work the VCR. She makes sure you have shampoo and toothpaste, and tells you to get yourself a key made. She does not, however, invite you up-stairs. This is her sanctuary, and when she is up there and wants to talk to you, she calls you on the house phone from her private line.

Mail for her comes to Jane Kachmer's business address. At Huntington Jane gave her a plastic bag full of it, and now, stand-ing at her kitchen counter, she goes through it summarily, each catalogue, complementary magazine subscription, birthday party invitation—in this case to a surprise party for *Friends'* Matt LeBlanc—passing through her hands only once. Only the most intelligent, respectful pieces of fan mail reach her. The rest is for-warded to the Gabrielle Reece Fan Club, presided over by Gabby's aunt Joanne, the sister of Gabby's deceased father, who sends members three small color pictures of Gabby and a key chain with a laminated picture of Gabby in her trademark black bikini, hugging a white volleyball to her chest.

Throughout Sunday afternoon and evening it is absolutely quiet. Gabby and Laird have sequestered themselves upstairs. Once Laird comes downstairs to go pick up some take-out food—hamburgers adorned with tomato slices as big as Frisbees and thick, shiny fries. Then he disappears upstairs again. Gabby doesn't come out of her room. Earlier in the day Laird said, "I have never seen her so tired, and I don't mean fatigue, I mean tired of all this."

Practice is at eleven on Monday morning, one hour before the deadline to cut players. At nine-thirty, there is still no sign of Gabby. Kim Crawford arrives with the beginnings of a cold, feverish and wringing her hands. Jen is downstairs in mascara and sweatpants, ready to go. No Gabby, also no Laird, who was scheduled to fly out to Hawaii today. Finally, he appears at around ten in swim trunks and a T-shirt and says that Gabby is not coming down (he, apparently, is not going to Hawaii until Wednesday). For the first time all summer she will not be going to practice. Kim and Jen are uneasy, careful not to trade glances. Reluctantly, they grab their gear and go.

Gabby is having The Working Woman's Nervous Breakdown, where, instead of getting to spend three months at a spa in Baden-Baden mending your shattered psyche, you get to sit in your bathrobe all day and let your hair get greasy. The next day it's back to the grind.

Kim and Jen return from practice around three. Kim leaves without saying anything. Jen says that practice did not go well. With Gabby missing, Coach Charlie put some high school girl in the middle, someone he knows from one of the clubs he coaches. Everyone on earth is not Gabby, but this girl was not Gabby to such a degree that it made practicing a near waste of time. But, Jen says, she was willing to make the best of it.

Kim, on the other hand, apparently went berserk. Not only did she blurt out that practice was *pointless* without Gabby, but when Jen suggested that Kim go up and block—you can't imagine the soft-spoken Jen doing anything as pointed as barking an order—Kim stomped off the court saying, "I don't even know what in the hell we're doing here!"

"You know," says Jen, "it's true, what everybody's been saying. That Gary gave Gab terrible advice at the start of the season. She didn't retain Katy Eldridge for this season, and last season she let Stephanie Cox go, and now they're all doing better than she is. I hope she's okay," says Jen, nodding upstairs, to where Gabby and Laird are still holed up. Later, I will find a note written on a green Post-it stuck to my bedside reading lamp: "Please don't read this the wrong way. I am very happy you are staying here, but I just have to get through some of this stuff, and I *will* get through this stuff, please just be patient and have a good time here. Love, G."

The next morning Jen is up and ready for practice at 8:30 A.M.

I said, "What's going on?" and she said, "Good news, I think. Or good news for me anyway. Kim's been cut, I'm back to hitting, and Julie Bremner—do you know Julie? She set for Gabby for a while last year. She's been gone on her honeymoon in Hawaii, but now she's back—is going to set." Jen went on to explain the logic: In Clearwater, Florida, and New York Nike had their best, most respectable performances of the season, with records of 3–1 and third-place finishes after playing in the semi-finals. With Katy Haller on the left, Jen on the right, Gabby in the center, and Julie setting, it's as close to that old team configuration as is possible at this point.

Gabby reappears as if nothing has happened, in her black running tights, a blue T-shirt, her hair pulled up in a high ponytail, mascara and lip gloss, looking like she always does before any other practice, well-groomed and a little distracted, like someone heading to work, and that night, after another promising practice, Laird makes a big dinner—marinated steaks, romaine salad with vinaigrette, corn on the cob. Laird likes to pray before a meal like this one, and instructs us all to thank the Lord for something, and we go around the table. Gabby thanks the Lord for her good health and Jen thanks the Lord for Gabby's immense strength—oh, and also for not allowing Gabby to cut her from the team—and I thank the Lord for Jen's sense of humor, and for a few moments everything is all right.

15

Being an Idiot

EVERYTHING A WOMAN DOES has an emotional component. Paying attention to my emotional side without surrendering to it is one of the toughest parts of playing professional sports. My coaches and trainer are working with me about getting over upsets. My trainer works with some professional hockey players and they seem to get over losses and screwups quicker. For me—for most female athletes I know—it's about tapping into your masculine side. It isn't natural for a woman to suffer disappointment and simply dismiss it with an "Oh, well, what's next?" We like to analyze it, experience all the emotions that are attached to it. There's nothing wrong with this, but if you've just gotten thrashed on the court, and you have an hour break and then you play again, you can't afford to linger. This has made me appreciate a guy's ability to get on with it. If it benefits me, I'll tuck my feminine side away for a while. I'll get my sports brain going. Once you figure out that you can tap into this masculine behavior and use it, then put it away again, you become more secure. You feel like you can appreciate your feminine side, your soft, emotional side, without feeling as if it might sabotage you when you know you need to be gnarly.

Frustration does not begin to cover my feelings about this season. I always felt the lack of team chemistry. Liane wound up doing better on another team, and maybe Christine and Jen would have also done better on another team. But no one can know that now.

I've played with Jennifer for years. People wonder why I kept refusing to cut her, but I knew that she had it in her to deliver. Midseason I took her aside and said, "Do not let me overshadow you." That's been a struggle for me. As a captain I'm responsible for creating an environment where my teammates perform up to their abilities, but I can't play the game for them.

I had this sense all season of waiting for the other shoe to drop. I kept finding out things it would have helped to have known earlier. After each roster change there was something else. After I drafted Julie Bremner to set, midseason, and she played a few games, she said to me, "You know, Christine and Jennifer say they want to get set more." I went to the next practice a little pissed off—"So the gossip is, you want to get set more. Why don't you tell me this so we can practice it?" Then we'd practice, all right, and I'd see them perform in practice but would never see it in a game. They'd get balls, no blocks, and suddenly it's 5-0—they'd hit it into the net or straight into the block, time after time after time. So I'd say to them, "Put yourselves in my shoes," and Jennifer said, "Well, you don't put every ball away." And I said, "No, but I am the go-to hitter. I touch every single ball." It got really brutal near the end. I thought, *Let them play with someone else.* I was forced to do a lot of cheerleading, but in the end I was very hard on them.

It was impossible. It seemed as if everything I learned in one tournament I had to relearn in the next one. I would try to motivate them, but then after a while, when they made critical mistake after critical mistake, I stopped saying anything. I didn't want to compound the situation. I basically tried to focus on my game. People at this level have to get themselves out of it—nothing I can say will help them.

My lowest moment of the season was St. Paul. The reality of the season was starting to set in. I was losing my essential optimism, which is necessary to be a successful competitor. If we'd won a tournament or went to a few finals . . . but it was becoming apparent that this wasn't going to happen. I was starting to think, *I've never gone through a season where I've never won a tournament.*

Sports isn't luck. It is about the talent, the persistence, and the personnel. The inner conflict of the team was wearing me down. Both Gary and Liane Sato were very resentful of Laird's presence during the season, but the problems I had with Liane were there from the beginning.

This year I did my killer circuit before the season, and we didn't win one tournament. You can't help but ask, "Is this worth it?" But the answer always is, "I have to do it this way or not at all." If you start saying, "This time I'll try harder, that time I won't," then you've already lost. If you can somehow perform at optimum levels all the time, that's the best way to do it. But you also have to be an idiot. You have to be willing not to analyze the situation, because the minute you start analyzing, you're finished. There's no money in professional beach volleyball, there's little respect—you've got to want to do it for some internal reason, having to do with your own demons. It's been said over and over again—I could make a gazillion dollars doing TV, or modeling, or movies. But I love volleyball. I love the way it makes me feel. I love that I can use my body to do something. No money, no amount of recognition has ever brought me the same feeling of accomplishment. Taking on a challenge, dealing with discomfort, sucking it up . . . all those things mean more to me than the rest. And I can say it and mean it because I've been on all sides of it. I've been recognized, I've been glamorized, I've made money. I'm not Michael Jordan, but I don't think you have to be at his level to understand that the issue is one of self-respect. My confidence comes from the fact that I know I'm capable, that I'm willing to roll up my sleeves and get down and dirty and uncomfortable and suffer and be sweaty and your nose is running and you need to spit and you've got sand between your teeth and up your butt—because that's real.

16

Seaside

DURING THE THREE-WEEK Olympic break Gabby has modified the team even further. In the three weeks between the 0–4 loss at Manhattan Beach and this weekend's tournament at Seaside, Oregon, Katie Haller was let go in favor of redrafting Christine "The Rocket" Romero. This is becoming so routine, I didn't bother to ask Gabby why she made the change. I know only the answer: that Katie didn't help the team win. And there, like a suitor waiting in the wings in some Restoration comedy, was the ever-present Christine, traveling as the alternate to all the midwestern stops, keeping the clock for each tournament, rarely losing that pleasantly goony smile of hers, looking killer in her short shorts, practicing, and waiting. To drop Katie and pick up Christine, Gabby exceeded the Monday noon trading deadline and she needed to get permission from the other captains to make the change. Every captain said no problem–the competitor in them wants Team Nike to be a real player–except Paul Mitchell captain Janet Cobb. She is leaving before the end of the season and had wanted to pick up Christine to replace herself.

After the grinding losses at both Huntington and Manhattan Beach, where Team Nike's record was 0–4, 0–4, Discus captain and Gabby's friend Stephanie Cox suggested as a joke that Gabby redraft Christine. This earned a grim laugh, the implication being that Nike could play musical teammates until the end of the season and nothing would change. Of course the biggest roster change, the one where Gabby jettisoned Liane and Gary, changed the complexion of the team so much that trying to work with Christine again wasn't such a bad idea. Even if redrafting her meant suffering the openmouthed reactions from everyone else on the tour—is Gabby nuts?

PORTLAND IS ALSO the hometown of Nike, with whom Gabby has an endorsement contract she's in the process of renegotiating, and she's busier than ever. She arrives the morning of the afternoon PLAY clinic, and goes directly to Nike headquarters where, at twelve-thirty, at the Bowdoins, one of the three restaurants on the Nike campus (a word that the people I know always say with invisible quotes; isn't it every grown man's dream never to leave college?), she has a Q & A with Nike employees. Afterward she meets briefly with founder and president Phil Knight, where she relates how difficult the season has been, how challenging it continues to be to put together a winning team, to trust her own judgment, to refrain from second-guessing all her changes, to develop as a captain as well as continue to develop as a player. . . .

Phil Knight is impressed with the magnitude of the failure and tries to put himself in the position of the corporation who paid $90,000 to sponsor a team. "Well," he says, "whose team is it?"

"Yours, Phil," says Gabby.

"And we drafted that badly!?" He is less astonished that he wasn't even aware that he "owned" Team Nike than that a team he owned should be struggling.

The next stop was NikeTown—the original one in downtown Portland—for the Q & A/raffle/autograph session/photo session that an official appearance consists of.

She is fifteen minutes late to NikeTown, a wonder of postmodern design that has a lot in common with a Victorian house—a collection of intimate rooms clustered around a less intimate room, a sort of foyer furnished with a cash register and big-screen overhead video monitor. This is great for putting the consumer in the mood to buy shoes, but terrible for any kind of personal appearance that draws more than the store's clerks, a handful of shoppers, and a few die-hards. Today, it's packed with a few hundred fans. Red paper raffle tickets are handed out as you enter. You might win a pair of Gabby's shoes—the big prize—or a T-shirt, poster, or water bottle—the standard stuff. Fans press forward in a crush around the empty black director's chair where she is supposed to sit. Fans line up in a row on the painted metal catwalk that connects two rooms on the second floor, the floor devoted to women's apparel. They slouch over the railing, elbow to elbow. The scene looks like something out of a prison movie.

A disc jockey from KFXX radio introduces himself as the "MC for the afternoon." Before Gabby appears, we are directed to turn our gaze to the big-screen overhead monitor, where they play *Gabbing with Gabby,* the now famous Nike video where shots of Gabby luxuriating in a T-shirt and bikini bottoms on a white satin sheet are intercut with her grunting, sweating, queen-of-kills routine. The MC's voice is BIG and the music emanating from the monitor is BIG and the lighting is dramatic. It's Fantasy on Parade without the parade. After the tape is finished, the lights dim and the music swells as if the Chicago Bulls are about to be introduced. The MC's voice goes deep DJ: "She's a model! She's a TV star! She's one of the most beautiful women in the world! Let's give it up for Gabrielle Reece!!"

Gabby appears in a black rayon T-shirt and red, black, and yellow Hawaiian print miniskirt.

"Let's sit down so you and I are on the same level," says the MC.

"That'll be the last time that'll happen."

Vintage Gabby. The witty, flirtatious insult.

"My story can be as boring or interesting as you want it to be," she begins. In lieu of giving a speech, she takes questions. A plaster cast of Michael Jordan, legs splayed, arm thrust out in a shoulder-dislocating reach for a plaster basketball that appears to be floating but is attached to his fingertips, is suspended over Gabby's head.

Someone asks, "What religion are you?"

Gabby retorts, "What's that got to do with it?"

Another person—one of those long-winded posers of questions who are a staple of Q & A's the world over, who invent questions in order to get off on their own erudition—asks what she feels about the tragedy at the Olympics and, more to the point, does it cause her any anxiety about competing in future Olympics?

It's a tedious question, more or less unanswerable ("I think the bombing was great! I hope to get a leg blown off in 2000!"), but not beyond the realm of concern. In fact, here at NikeTown, in humble Portland, Oregon, there is more security for her than there was in New York or Chicago. There is Junior, who looks like a tight end turned bodyguard, and an officious, thick-necked guy who keeps trying to press us back into the crowd after the appearance. He wears a pale blue shirt with darker blue stripes, buttoned closed at the neck.

"Miss Reece is coming through this way," he says.

"We're with Gab," I say.

"No more autographs," he says.

"We're with Gabby."

"You need to move back."

When I take out my notebook and begin to make notes, he relents.

FROM THE APPEARANCE to the clinic, at Pioneer Courthouse Square. It's one of those disorientingly hot August days that Portland gets a half-dozen days a year. It's not smothering like the Midwest or searing like SoCal, but a combination of both, humid and glary, relentless, especially in the brick amphitheater that is Pioneer Courthouse Square.

At around 4:20 a group of about seventy-five kids in black

PLAY T-shirts, sleeves rolled up to their shoulders, begin trickling in. Odwalla, the juice maker who specializes in sludgy vegetable and fruit juices, has a booth; the ubiquitous Sony AutoSound semi is here, parked on the north side of the square. At 4:30, when the clinic is supposed to start, a clutch of protesters appear. They carry a white banner that says JUSTICE FOR JOBS! and there is a collective moment of consternation: Is this a demonstration against Nike? But no, it's about a local department store, and their apparent unfair treatment of the Canadians who stitch their men's suits.

The clinic is held on something called a sport court. It looks like a large gymnastics mat bisected by a net. When Team Nike is introduced, the announcer calls setter Julie Romius née Bremner "the newest member of the team," but also seems to want to call redraftee Christine Romero the same thing: ". . . out of Long Beach State, the newest . . . no, wait, I already said that . . . the rookie Christine 'The Rocket' Romero!"

SEASIDE, OREGON, WHERE the tenth stop in the tour is held, is not around the block from Portland the way they make it sound in the program. It's seventy-four miles away, down a two-lane highway that tunnels through the forest and over the coast range, past a single Dairy Queen, a single mom-and-pop grocery that sells worms and espresso, and two restaurants, Oney's (marked with a giant, black-bearded lumberjack that looks like Bluto from the old Popeye cartoons) and Camp 18.

Seaside itself is homely and a little seedy. There are pedal-driven surreys for rent and an aquarium past its prime. Several years ago a madman tried to kidnap Victor, the aquarium's lone lobster, who was almost forty years old. A guard chased the madman, who dropped Victor, cracking his shell. The aquarium had Victor stuffed and stuck up on the wall.

The beach where the tournament is held is "At the Lewis & Clark Trail Turnaround," advertised with a marker. There is some doubt about whether this is the exact spot where Lewis & Clark actually turned around, or whether the Seaside city fathers are taking advantage of the fact that this was the general stretch of ocean where L & C ran into the dead end of the Pacific.

By noon, when Team Nike is set to play their first match, it's still chilly and overcast. Overhead a white blimp with red tail and trim hovers in the pale grayish white sky, nearly camouflaged. It's for a product called RUSH: The High Speed Tanning Accelerator, a must-have in this climate.

Even though this is Friday, traditionally the day when the bleachers are studded with a few lone spectators, today they're nearly full of northwesterners bundled up in the flannel shirts and plaid woolen anoraks that will never go out of style up here. On the top row of bleachers opposite the Invited Guests Section, two girls huddle in brightly colored sleeping bags. The large crowd is due to an amateur volleyball tournament, the Fifteenth Annual Seaside Beach Volleyball Tournament, also sponsored by Bud Light. The paper said the organizers expected about 3,000. There are also an unknown number of representatives from Nike, who, in their flannel and wool caps, are indistinguishable from more ordinary fans. Tinker Hatfield, with whom Gabby designs her cross-trainers, is there with his wife; Sue Levin, the head of women's sports marketing, is there with her boyfriend and her dog, whose leash keeps getting tangled around the legs of the folding chairs.

Gabby, dressed in a khaki sweatshirt and her black Lycra tights, which she's worn in every game, is subdued but cheerful. It's cold this early in the morning, in the mid-forties, with fog so dense you can't even see the water. Once again, she is trying out a new team.

Liane-Jen-Christine-Gabby begat Liane-Jen-Kim-Gabby begat Julie-Jen-Kim-Gabby begat Julie-Jen-Katie-Gabby has finally begotten Julie-Jen-Christine (again)-Gabby. After this weekend there are only three matches left. The musical chairs can't go on forever presumably, but then again, they can. What was once alarming is now commonplace. The trick is to not let losing become equally commonplace—even at this late date.

Gabby reports that last night, at one, she received a phone call. Laird answered and the caller threatened first to break her legs, then kill her. The temptation is to not take this seriously, but we all know this kind of thing needs to be taken very seriously, and when a vintage northwestern oddball finds a place in the bleachers, the morning turns ominous. The weirdo wears a green khaki army jacket limp with grime, a navy blue stocking cap pulled down almost to the bridge of his nose, a pair of amber-tinted ski goggles, and black ski gloves. He has a thin brown mustache and arranges himself with care on the top row of the bleachers nearest the Invited Guests Section, where Gabby has been waiting before warm-ups.

ROUND 3, GAME 1. Team Nike versus Team Discus.

As Nike hops out to a 4–1 lead, I scan the bleachers. They're the most crowded they've ever been this early in the tournament. I'm hard-pressed to think of another athlete of Gabby's caliber who is this available to the crowd, who is so unprotected from the fans, admirers, and weirdos her beauty, talent, and celebrity attract. There are no tickets, no way to weed out people who attend with purpose from aimless sorts just wandering by, looking for something to do. There are no metal detectors; anyone in the bleachers could have a gun.

At 8:13 the score is 4–1 Nike; at 5:54 the score is 8–4 Discus. The unsinkable Christine Romero looks strong, and yet . . . and yet. Soon it is 13–4 Discus; the final score will be 15–5. Nike cannot afford to score so few points; low points have kept them from the semis in the past, and will do so this weekend as well.

Coach Charlie Brand sits forward in his folding chair, elbows on his knees. Jen is serving and he is yelling, "Hit it *hard,* hit it *hard."* Jen's serves tend to get weaker and weaker as the team falls farther and farther behind. This time, however, she aces one serve. The next she sends straight into the net.

ROUND 5, GAME 2. Team Nike versus Team Sony.

Nike has their usual problems—slow feet. Charlie, from the sidelines, yells at Christine and Julie: "GO, don't LOOK!" Again, Nike leaps out to a 4–1 lead. At 7–5 Nike, Sony takes a sand time-out. Team Nike is cautiously amped; that chaos-under-control feeling, itchy and hectic, spreads through the team. *We are ahead, we are still ahead.* Each service is critical; each impossible up must be made possible. Charlie: "Hands OUT. Focus!"

Sony makes five straight points, and soon Nike falls behind, 7–10. The feeling of possibility evaporates. Bad luck, bad calls, and almost great playing don't add up. Nike can't absorb the usual ups and downs of the game; they've got to play brilliantly to compensate for the lack of experience they've had as a team. The strong moments that come and bring with them the possibility of success must be woven together, a rope of strong moments, one after the next. Gabby drops a few little kills over the net, placed just so. She rolls one, kills one, keeps wrestling the side out back to her team. Charlie, during a sand time-out late in the game: "We're in it! We're in it! We're in it!" But they aren't; Sony wins, 15–10.

Charlie delivers a brief pep talk and the team breaks. Gabby steps outside the dugout and the autographing begins. Always the autographing, always the picture taking. Win or lose, rain or shine, snit or no snit. At this moment, it's definitely snit. Gabby is frustrated with setter Julie and her set selection. "I'm fighting my own team!" says Gabby to no one in particular.

ROUND 8, GAME 3. Team Nike versus Team Norelco.

For the third time in this week's tournament, Nike is up 4–1 early in the game.

Soon it is 9–1, *Nike's biggest lead of the season.*

Nike manages to dominate, but every rally is a war. It has

always been a war, but for some reason Team Nike, in all its incarnations, has refused to accept this. Once, in New York, before the seasonlong tailspin, when Nike ground out an ugly win against Sony to advance to the semis, Gabby herself said, "It's so DIFFICULT, why does it have to be so damn difficult?" Because it is, and the other teams, perhaps lesser teams in terms of raw talent, have known this, and they have fought the war, and they have become better warriors, until it no longer looks like such a battle and is back to resembling a game.

Nike hangs on. It's 10–4. Then 12–8. Charlie goes, "C'mon! Hands, hands, elbows, elbows. GO . . . GET . . . THE BALL!" Norelco is creeping back in, but Nike manages to hang in there. It's a grovel-a-thon, not beautiful beach volleyball, the kind that makes highlight reels, the kind that CE prez Craig Elledge would use to woo new team sponsors. The ball hops and caroms here and there, kept alive by a forearm or a panicky little set. One of Nike's passes is so unseemly that Team Norelco turns its collective back to the net—getting in position for the next play—when Gabby rolls the ball up and over. It dribbles to the sand on Norelco's side, a point for Nike.

The score is 12–10 Nike, then 13–10 Nike. At match point for Nike the side out goes back and forth, back and forth, then the clock is at forty-two seconds; then Christine "The Rocket" Romero launches a ridiculously miscalculated sky ball meant to waste a few seconds. It goes crazily out of bounds, but it's a measure of Christine's confidence and daring that she attempts it at all. Later, I will tell her, "You know, you're like the unsinkable

Molly Brown," to which her response will be, "Really? Cool! Who's that?"

Nike wins by the clock, 14–11. It's the first win after–what– eight straight losses? The last time they won was in St. Paul; they went 0–4 at Huntington, 0–4 at Manhattan Beach. The longest losing streak in the league is now broken. As the afternoon progresses, the odd weather continues, fog coming and going, obscuring the ocean. People spend a goodly amount of time trying to decide whether they're freezing or roasting. A scant three or four miles inland, it's 100 degrees. We are in any case getting sunburned. We feel it on our cheeks.

ROUND 10, GAME 4.

Nike is set to play the final match of the day, against first-place Team Paul Mitchell, who, with their 3–0 record, are going straight to the finals tomorrow. The match is set for five, but doesn't get under way until six. As they take the sand, Nike in black tights and white sports bras that blend in with the cold white sky, that also match the white RUSH suntan lotion blimp that's been hovering overhead all day, it begins to drizzle. Standing room only, the crowd presses in, the pale sky, the sweaty dampness, the end of the day, the drizzle. The Worst Team against The Best Team, with many important persons from the corporation that sponsors The Worst Team in attendance.

What is at stake here is the perception of Gabrielle Reece as a marquee athlete. In 1997 this is the way it is for most world-class athletes; almost any athlete you see on a commercial or a billboard makes more money being in the commercial or on the billboard than he or she does being in the paint, the end zone, or on third.

Gabby's relationship with Nike has not been uncomplicated. First of all, women spend more on athletic footwear and apparel than men do, yet Nike's female athletes still play second fiddle to their male athletes. This isn't sexism; the simple reality is that until very recently women's sports have not proved as lucrative as men's.

"We looked at ourselves in the mirror and decided that in a lot of areas we are still thought of as a men's company," explained Nike spokeswoman Robin Carr in a newspaper interview. "We're trying to create role models that high school girls can look up to, because they are our future." Still, volleyball is handled by the woman who promotes cheerleading at Nike.

"I do a great job for them," says Gabby. "But the problem is, if you give 120 percent you're going to ask for 120 percent, and people don't like that. Particularly when a woman does it. If a male athlete asks for everything he feels he needs to preserve his self-respect, he's called a good businessman; if a female athlete does it, she's called difficult, demanding, and bitchy."

Second, until this year, Nike had yet to make beach volleyball a priority, preferring to concentrate on more visible women's sports such as basketball and soccer. While Nike puts their efforts where they anticipate most immediate results, they still cast a wide net over the entire ocean of human activity. From Brazilian soccer to college cheerleading, the swoosh is there. At last year's Montreal International Comedy Festival, described by *The New Yorker* as "the Cannes of comedy" (where, in the past, both Brett Butler and Tim Allen were discovered), Nike sent someone to pass out shoes to the comedians who emerged from the festival as the Flavors of the Month.

But things are changing. Nike has decided to step up their commitment to beach volleyball. Although the plans are yet to be finalized, there's been talk of the first World Championship of Beach Volleyball, to be held in the fall of 1997. Nike Sports Entertainment will produce the event and Nike will be the primary sponsor. Patterned after big tennis grand slams like the U.S. Open and Wimbledon, the tournament would pit country against country and feature not just doubles, but also fours. For the first time, men's and women's prize money will be equal.

NIKE GETS OUT to a fast start, part of their new personality. Their old personality, as we know, was getting left in the dust, never able to make it back into the game. Then, usually, when they were so far down they had no hope of winning, they began playing better, looser, more confident. Sometimes they simply gave up. But this time, they're out 4–1, and then, in a few ticks of the clock, it's all tied up again.

Then it goes like this:

Nike delivers a kill, and they go up 5–4, then 6–4.
Teams change sides. Nike 6 serving 4.

Side out.
Paul Mitchell 4 serving 6. Point, Paul Mitchell. 5–6.
Side out.
Nike 6 serving 5. Point, Nike. 7–5.
Side out.
Paul Mitchell 5 serving 7. Point, Paul Mitchell. 6–7.
Side out.
Nike 7 serving 6.
Side out.
Paul Mitchell 6 serving 7.
6:33 minutes left to play.
Side out.
Nike 7 serving 6.
Side out.
Paul Mitchell 6 serving 7. Point, Paul Mitchell. All tied up, 7–7.
Side out.
Nike 7 serving 7. Point, Nike. 8–7.
Side out.
Paul Mitchell 7 serving 8.
Side out.
Nike 8 serving 7. Point, Nike. 9–7. Point, Nike. 10–7.
Side out.
Paul Mitchell 7 serving 10.
Side out.
Nike 10 serving 7. Nike–net violation.
Side out.
Paul Mitchell 7 serving 10. Point, Paul Mitchell. 8–10.
Side out.
Nike 10 serving 8.
Side out.
Paul Mitchell 8 serving 10. Point, Paul Mitchell. 9–10.
Side out.
Nike 10 serving 9. Point, Nike. 11–9.

Sand time-out. Paul Mitchell setter Missy Kurt needs a medical time-out to have her jaw adjusted. It's popped. Or something.

Nike 11 serving 9. Point, Nike. 12–9.
Side out.
Paul Mitchell 9 serving 12.
Side out.
Nike 12 serving 9.
Side out.
Paul Mitchell 9 serving 12.
Side out.
Nike 12 serving 9.
Side out.
Paul Mitchell 9 serving 12.
Side out.
Nike 12 serving 9.
Side out.
Paul Mitchell 9 serving 12. Point, Paul Mitchell. 10–12.
3:34 minutes left to play.
Paul Mitchell 10 serving 12.
Side out.
Nike 12 serving 10. Point, Nike. 13–10.
Side out.
Paul Mitchell 10 serving 13.
Side out.
Nike 13 serving 10.
Side out.
Paul Mitchell 10 serving 13. Point, Paul Mitchell. 11–13.
Paul Mitchell 11 serving 13.
Side out.
2:35 minutes left to play.
Nike 13 serving 11. Point, Nike. 14–11.
Nike 14 serving 11. Match point.
Side out.

Paul Mitchell 11 serving 14. Point, Paul Mitchell. 12–14.
1:55 minutes left to play.
Paul Mitchell 12 serving 14.
Side out.
Nike 14 serving 12. Match point. Point, Nike. 15–12.

Is it joy or simply relief? Victory, yes. But they still don't
have the points to make the semifinals. Victory, but also frustration.

17

Anyone Can Suck It Up
for Forty-five Minutes

I HAVE THE MOTIVATION to be fit because I'm an example. I'm representing the sport, my peers, women's sports, myself. The reality is, I need to look the part. I need to be visually convincing. A lot of female athletes are in awesome shape, but unless the Everyman consumer sees the muscles and the leanness and the low body fat, they don't believe it. It's ironic, because I am authentic in my pursuits and abilities and way of trying to be in the world, but the fact of it isn't enough. It's got to look right. People have to see the stomach muscles, the biceps, the tight legs, the veins. This is not to say that it's all cosmetic. My body is such that if I just do the work it comes out that way.

But not everyone can do this, and it's important if you want to train or to look a certain way to know your body. For example, me. Large gluteus maximus muscle, strong upper legs, thin lower legs, biceps that develop easily, back and shoulders that take more work. Everyone has muscles that pump up easier than others.

Before you do anything, you've got to know what you are. "I'm 6' with a small waist." "I'm 5'5" with a square build." You have to be realistic. You can't be some strong stocky girl with a large waist, broad shoulders, a flat butt, and thin legs and look at some curvaceous girl and think, *That's what I want to look like.* You must work with what you've been given. You must.

You need to know why you want to do it. If it's because you want to please your boyfriend, then be prepared for when you break up—there goes your boyfriend AND your motivation. Is it because you want to look a certain way? Okay, but in the end that won't get your butt into the gym five, six days a week either. When I kick in, it's three days on, one day off, three days on, six days a week.

If it's to feel better, to find a place in which to funnel some energy, then going to the gym is enough. If you're an athletic girl or woman, if your fitness level is meant to enhance either your soccer game or your tennis game at the club, let's say, then you've got to educate yourself about your sport. Your training has to be geared toward what you're doing in your sport as well as creating a balanced body. In volleyball, for example, there's a lot of jumping. At one point in your jump you're very strong, but at another point you're very weak. When you get into the gym, your job is to work on strengthening the weak part because the strong part is being sustained while you're playing.

There are valid reasons to want to change the way you look. For me, I compete better when I'm heavier. In 1994, I played in the best shape I've been in in my life. You could see every muscle in my chest and my arms. I was in impeccable shape. I weighed 161 pounds. But I got injured. I appeared to be ripped/skinny, but I wasn't in command. I like it when I'm heavier. I feel stronger, more powerful, more dominant. I feel meaner.

There can be a mixture of motivations, too. For me, there are three. I feel better, I like the idea of the working hard thing—when I come out of the gym after breaking my ass I feel worthy of living and breathing and walking around—and, absolutely, enhancement of athletic performance. When I am doing my circuit I don't care about anything besides becoming a better athlete. The circuit is too hard. Nothing else could get me there. You could tell me, "Gabrielle, you could squeeze your butt cheeks and there would be no fat there, none, nada," and I'd say, "Not worth it."

As I woman I like looking fit, but it is calculated. If I didn't genetically have good stomach muscles, I would probably work very hard on them so that they would be strong and look the part. Already I don't look the part unless you take my clothes off and get me in motion.

I hear this from women all the time, especially girls in college: "I don't want to lift because I don't want to get too big." I have a hard time with that because they don't know what they are saying. You don't just "get big," you don't do two sets of leg presses and are miraculously transformed into a German speed skater. It takes paying a lot of attention to your diet and the kind of lifting you're doing. It's very specific. And anyway, if you're a short girl with a tendency to have big legs, why not go for it? Why not make them as hard and as powerful as you possibly can? Why insist on thinking it's better to be a beanpole?

The other thing I don't like about this fear of being big is that it feeds into the general female thing of wanting to be less—less powerful, less assertive, less demanding, less opinioned, less present, less big. High school girls are a little more easy about that, but college girls, from around eighteen to twenty-one, start on this thing: "I don't want my traps to get too big." To which I say, "Okay, but then don't expect your body to be a sculpted masterpiece, because that only happens through lifting."

THE MYTH OF THE SALAD. The number-one fear of girls is cellulite, got to be. They say, "I'm just going to run and eat salad." The problem with that is the human body is so smart that if you're not giving it enough to survive—and a salad is basically nothing but crunchy water—the message "I'm starving!" goes out and anything you put in your mouth it holds on to. So you could wind up screwing up your metabolism, not being able to burn any fat, because your body is holding on to everything. So people who exercise but don't eat aren't doing anything. You're never going to get a hard body if you don't eat protein, period. Chicken, egg whites, supplements. You're never going to have firm triceps if you don't lift weights.

I can eat anything I want and burn it. When I was really ripped I ate very very healthfully. I go back and forth. This morning I ate egg whites and brown rice; if I feel like a cheeseburger, than I'll eat a cheeseburger. But I'm also willing to work hard.

This wasn't always the case. When I was in college, I wasn't very strong. I used to skip workouts because I didn't feel like it. Now I've gotten to the place where "I just don't feel like it" is no longer part of my vocabulary. My advice to women: Take the emotion out of it.

18

Hermosa

AT 9:30 A.M., before the first game begins, Gabby grabs me before I find my usual courtside folding chair and says, "Go and rap with Aunt Norette," then points to a lone woman sitting in the middle of the bleachers on the opposite side of the court. Even from this distance across the court I can tell she is a little ill at ease in her long-sleeved denim top and long pants, perched uncomfortably on the edge of the wooden seat.

Norette and Joe Zucarello, who raised Gabby from the age of three and a half to seven, have flown in from Phoenix for the tournament. Norette is one of two short, voluble "aunts" in Gabby's life—the other is Aunt Joanne. Both are around 5'2", which means they began looking up at Gabby when she was seven years old.

Norette and Joe grew up with Gabby's mother. Terry lived around the corner from Joe, who met and fell in love with Norette when they were all fifteen years old. Terry and Norette became friends because they shared a typical teenaged girl condition: Both were unhappy and both loved to read. Aunt Norette and Uncle Joe are the kind of people who, even though you are all grown up, you need to call Aunt and Uncle. They are loud, warm, and hilariously stubborn. When I ask Joe if he wants some sunscreen he says, "Nah! I'm Sicilian!" When I ask Norette if she wants sunscreen she says, "Nah! We live in Phoenix!" At the end of the day, they are both walking Solarcaine ads.

In 1972, when Terry asked Norette to watch Gabby, or Gaba, as she was called, Norette believed it was for a month at most. "The weeks turned into years," says Norette. "I had suddenly given birth to a three-year-old." Joe was an aluminum siding installer and Norette stayed home with Gaba. They had no children of their own. They treated Gaba to an action-packed (if you are a child) working-class life, and Norette still has the embarrassing memories and fuzzy Instamatic snapshots to prove it: Gabby on a fishing trip wearing a baby blue T-shirt that says SEC-OND MATE GABA in iron-on letters, holding a line with a twisting fish on it away from her legs, a mixture of curiosity and repulsion on her face; Gabby diving off a diving board at a community pool; Gabby looking surly but dutiful, posing in a pink tutu; Gabby standing cheek by jowl with a prizewinning head of broccoli. Trips to wild animal parks and ice cream parlors, camping trips and slumber parties. Girlfriends to build clubhouses with. Regular bedtime. Chores.

"We gave her security when she needed it," says Norette, "but she gave us so much more. She was our child."

She tells me the now infamous story, not generally known, but known by everyone close to Gabby, how one day when Gabby was seven Terry phoned out of the blue and told Norette she wanted Gabby back. Gabby stood on the sofa and cried.

"Of course, we tried with a lawyer," says Norette, "but there was nothing to be done. I put her on that plane, and Joe at that time was out of work, and that same week he got an offer in Anchorage, Alaska, doing siding, and we boarded up our house, the one we lived in with Gabby, and got in our Datsun and drove to Alaska. We took our dog, a white Samoyed named Daisy by Gabby—the other choice was Ballerina, odd, since Gabby hated taking ballet. I didn't talk to Gabby for a full year. I worried and cried every single day of that year, wondering what had happened to her, where she was and how she was. It's a cliché, but I gotta say it. It was like losing an arm."

Norette owns a mother's memories of Gabby. "She was in the drum and bugle corps, only it wasn't called that. It was called precision marching, with tall flag. Their group was called the Peanuts. Did we think that was a laugh riot."

Aunt Joanne and Uncle Peter and their children arrive at Hermosa carrying a pink bakery box brimming with Cuban meat pies. Aunt Joanne introduces Norette to a friend of one of their daughters as someone "Gabby stayed with for a while when she was little." The party in the bleachers begins.

Christine Romero's family is there as well, sitting in a clump a few yards away. They are proactive cheerleaders; in the beat of silence just after Christine has launched one of her spectacular jumping serves but before she's punched the ball, her mother has an interesting habit of shrieking "Christine! I believe in you!"

The aunts and uncles of Gabby are reactive. Norette isn't quite sure how the game works—but every time Nike fumbles the ball or whacks one straight into the net, Norette wails. "Oh, nooooooooooooo. . . ."

"Get back in, Nike. Side out," yells one of Gabby's nieces.

"It's impossible," says Norette. "The other team. They're everywhere. Oh, noooooooo. . . ."

During a time-out, an old Stones tune rocks across the beach and Uncle Peter stands up and starts shaking it. Spectators in the vicinity clap and someone says, "Look out, Laker girls."

The music stops, but Peter doesn't. As the game resumes, he's still standing and issues this directive: "Nike! Let's zip in and zap!"

One long serve is followed by another. Gabby fluffs a few kills.

The cheering Romeros are specific to an embarrassing degree. "C'mon, Nike, let's get this serve IN."

Norette wails, "This is awful. No. I'll tell myself it's good for her character. I'll tell myself that. She's so used to winning, this is good. Oh, noooooooooo. . . ."

Nike loses, Gabby is fuming, slapping sand from herself, throwing handfuls on her feet. It ends with her sending the ball straight into the net.

"We LOVE you, Nike!" yells Aunt Norette.

Just after the game has ended and the next teams are on the court warming up, Terry arrives at the Invited Guests Section with her usual exasperating timing. She is wearing blue shorts and a white T-shirt, looking like any girl bound for a day at the beach. Norette and Joe haven't seen Terry since Gabby graduated from high school eight years ago. Norette sees her across the court, her face hidden by her long blond hair. Now Norette fumes, her hands tucked into fists.

Team Nike plays Team Norelco for their final game of the day and, as it turns out, the tournament. Norelco sprints out to a 7–0 lead, and for the first time this season there is a sense of terminal defeat about Team Nike's performance. There are only two more tournaments after this one, in San Diego and Santa Cruz, and it looks as if maybe they're just waiting for the whole thing to be over. They can show up the next weekend and then the next, and then it's over. Or maybe Gabby is a little rattled because her whole complicated family has shown up today.

When the score reaches 8–0, Norette yells, "Don't worry, Gaba! Some days you eat the bear, some days the bear eats you!"

THEN UNCLE JOE annoys Aunt Norette by going over to the Invited Guests Section to say hello to Terry. He eventually winds up sitting next to her, having pulled up a stray folding chair and tucked himself in beside her at the end of the first row. When you look at them across the court, they seem able to talk as if nothing happened; or perhaps all their talk is masking the fact that something enormous has happened.

Norette says, "He makes me so mad. He's just doing that to show that he's a bigger person than I am. Well, I've largely forgiven Terry for what she did, but there's one thing I can't forget. Before Gabby left I gave her a photo album I'd put together with all the pictures I'd taken while she was with us so she could remember. Last December I asked Gabby if she still had it and she said no, that somewhere along the way it had been lost."

By the end of the day, Nike is 0–4, a great disappointment, especially after the final two games the week before at Seaside. This is the first time Uncle Joe and Aunt Norette have seen Gabby play in person. "It's agonizing," says Norette, "much worse than watching it on TV."

THAT NIGHT, THE TEAM DINNER is at Gabby's house. Although she does cook, likes to cook, she is wise enough to know that under this kind of stress it's wiser to expend less energy, and so Laird goes out and brings back a honey-baked ham, white containers of coleslaw and baked beans, and biscuits.

Uncle Peter and Uncle Joe sprawl on the huge beige sectional in the family room; the kids play backgammon in the living room. Jen Meredith sits with Aunt Norette and me at Gabby's large pine dining room table, looking through old albums, all covered with calico fabric, lovingly edged in lace. Aunt Norette, archivist by calling if not by trade, has dutifully included every snapshot, even those that are out of focus and highly unflattering. Jen looks through the album and says, "Why doesn't Gabby ever look like a dork? I mean, where are all the pictures with the frosted pink lipstick and fuzzy sweaters?"

Norette frets about Gabby. "She'll be in a bad mood tonight. She's so competitive."

I said, "No, she'll be hilarious. She's one of those people who's funniest when she's most frustrated."

Norette says that she's like that, and tells me how, once, ten years ago she felt a lump in her stomach and took herself to the doctor.

"I never go to the doctor. I say if you don't have a thing wrong with you, and you want something to be wrong with you, go to a doctor." The lump was diagnosed as a hernia. She was scheduled for surgery, but after the anesthesia wore off and she woke up, she felt her abdomen and felt no incision, no stitches. "Turns out I had a tumor on my ovary. Ovarian cancer it was. I was scared to death, day after day after day, morning to night. The only time I wasn't scared was when I was asleep. But the thing was, I was never funnier. I had everyone screaming with laughter—Joe, the nurses and doctors, everyone. If I was to write a book it would be about that—how to laugh your way through cancer."

Later I mention this to Gabby, how maybe her fortitude isn't completely the product of genetics. She says, "Aunt Norette is killer. No doubt about that."

THE PENULTIMATE TOURNAMENT of the season is in San Diego, and for the first time all summer Laird won't be there. For a segment of *The Extremists,* for which Laird is now a correspondent, he has entered a paddleboard race across the Catalina Channel, the thirty-two-mile stretch of choppy Pacific that runs between Catalina Island and the Southern California coast.

Like most self-made women, Gabby has honed her naturally independent nature so that she is more than capable of getting herself to where she needs to be, performing her appointed task and suffering the sting of defeat or the pinch-me joys of triumph without support. Unlike many self-made women, however, she easily acknowledges that while she can technically do it alone, she wouldn't be doing it half as well were it not for the people around her. "You got to have a good camp," she says, "you got to have help. And I do." She is strong enough and politically blasé enough to admit she needs her man. Having Laird with her throughout the long, losing season was key, she said. "He helped turn the goose eggs into flowers quicker. I was able to come to every tournament, loss after loss after loss, and be tough and competitive as opposed to tough and vindictive."

Gabby assumes that Laird's cross-channel paddle will be business as usual. Surfers of Laird's caliber aren't just great at catching waves, dude, they also have arms and shoulders as strong and reliable as German machinery. They can propel themselves and their boards through the surf for hours on end; part of Laird's workout often includes taking one of his long boards out for a three-hour paddle. So Gabby is not worried.

San Diego is reputed to have the finest weather in North America—the average year-round temperature is seventy-five degrees—and today the city is travel-brochure beautiful. The beach scene is all primary colors—blue ocean, yellow sand, the cheeks and shoulders of beachgoers red with sunburn.

Whether it's the lack of Laird or general end-of-the-season malaise, Gabby is a bit edgy. Her mother is here and has done something touchingly curious. Terry has painted several banners that say things like GO NIKE GO! and GO GABBY! The banners are illustrated with leaping dolphins. Gabby is surprised and embarrassed to see this homespun display of support and asks her mother to take them down.

The tournament begins as usual. Team Nike loses their first two games, but near the end of the third game something happens. The score is 11–10, and Gabby is in a familiar predicament. Nike needs to win this one to make the semifinals.

Diving to get a ball, Gabby stumbles into the barricade. The long low strip of sponsor banners is held in place by a metal structure, a series of poles that extend diagonally from the horizontal top pole, over which the banners are draped. Gabby knows immediately that she's banged her knee, but it's only after she's dusted the sand from herself and trotted back to the game that referee Rick Olmstead tells her to get over to medical.

"Forget it, Rick, I'm fine."

But she is not fine. The gash inflicted by the edge of one of the poles is so deep that at the center of the wound you glimpse a wink of bone. At the hospital, where Gabby is eventually taken, it takes longer for the doctor to pick out bits of aluminum than it does to sew the fifteen stitches. Gabby's leg is wrapped from shin to thigh and she finds herself suddenly on the disability list.

There is one last boat to Catalina that Saturday evening, and rather impulsively (by Gabby's standards) she decides to take it out to the island on the off chance she'll be able to catch one of the dinghies accompanying Laird and the rest of the paddle-boarders on their glide across the channel. She finds a place on the gray inflatable Zodiac–basically a fancy raft–with *The Extremists* soundman, the vessel that will travel closest to Laird.

But what promised to be a more or less routine event–Laird, remember, has also paddled across the English Channel, a far more unfriendly strip of water–turns out to be a grueling seven-and-a-half-hour schlep.

The current is stronger than expected, the water colder. Laird has been provided with the wrong kind of board and even the wrong kind of shirt. For a paddleboard race of this length the paddlers are given mesh shirts to protect their chests from getting rubbed raw. Laird's shirt is too big and by the end of the race—in which he comes in a disappointing eighth—one of his nipples is bleeding.

"For hours I bobbed up and down in that Zodiac, calling through a megaphone over the side to him, 'You can do it, baby.' It was terrible to watch, but I was glad suddenly that I'd gotten injured. It allowed me to be there for my mate, who, at that moment, needed me a lot more than my team did."

19

The Catch, the Edge

ONE OF THE THINGS I believe most strongly is that it's important to develop your mind, not simply for the sake of knowledge but for the sense of security it gives you. You know you can get from here to there. For me, I know that if we talk I can probably engage in the conversation, or at least ask intelligent questions, and if a situation comes up, I can probably deal with it. There's a tremendous amount of security in that. It's the same with sports. When you are playing at the highest level you can play at, it doesn't matter if anyone else is better than you are. I love watching other people play good volleyball because I know what I can do. My game may be different, but I can still appreciate their game.

We all have personal missions in life. Mine is not

so different from most people's—finding and maintaining peace of mind. The catch is that for me that means constantly challenging myself. If I don't have some sort of personal challenge every day, I'm a nightmare to live with. Beyond that, I'm always working to empty myself out of all the stuff that I don't need, whether it be emotional baggage, preconceived notions, or wrong attitudes. It's like my closet—I clean it out every single month. The clothes I'm not wearing I get rid of. Everything needs to be in use—always.

Enduring my youth, with its tests, including living with my physical size, has paid off tenfold. Even though I had so many problems with my mother, one of the great gifts she gave me was the fact that she was so accepting of her own size. She was always erect, as though being a 6'2" woman was completely normal. Being that tall when she was a girl was much harder than it was for me, than it is now. Uncle Joe said that when my mother would walk through the neighborhood she would never meet your gaze. Her eyes may have been cast down, but she never ever slouched.

Because I am so tall, there are rules that I have never been able to conform to. Doesn't matter whether I'm a businesswoman or an athlete or a telephone operator. I would never be able to be cute and little and meek, never. So I just thought, *Okay, why not go all the way?* When I was modeling people thought I was on glue. "Why are you playing *volleyball*? You have a chance to make a lot of money."

This year was critical for me. Last year I sort of felt like I knew what I was doing, but this year, despite the fact we never won a tournament, never came close to winning a tournament, I KNEW, I finally knew, what I was doing. The situation was so bad, but I could still reach the level of play I wanted to without any support. I could still put the ball where I wanted to even under the worst of circumstances. It's a nice place to arrive at.

But I never want to lose my edge. It's one of the real pitfalls of the rich and famous thing. The second you start thinking that you're too good to pick up your own dry cleaning, you've lost it. People become uninterested in you and you've lost your edge. When you've lost your edge, you're a finished story. The ending is known.

It's also the secret of having a healthy, living, breathing relationship—that desire to keep your edge, to be an interesting person. Women who think, *I got my man,*

I got my kid, now I'm going to hang out in the comfort zone, those are the women who get left. I don't ever want to be a woman who got left because I got comfortable. I want children, but I don't want children in order to fill up what I perceive to be holes in my life. I will always have outside interests, and every woman should. Every woman should have something to talk about when she sits down at the dinner table. She should have a point of view, an opinion—it's part of why her man was intrigued in the first place, if he's any kind of man—and women sometimes lose sight of this.

People on the outside sometimes wonder if there is a lot of jealousy of me on the tour, if that isn't in fact part of the problem. There will always be people who are jealous, to greater and lesser degrees, but mostly I don't think the other players have the audacity to be jealous of me. I've been around for a few years, taken my knocks. No one would ever say, after this season, that I'm just some pretty girl who can't think of anything better to do with her time.

My biggest challenge this season was to continue to lead, even when things weren't going as well as I would have liked them to. Sometimes I had to be unreasonable, or unfair, and that was difficult. But standing up for anything in life means setting yourself up to have people against you. This is a source of conflict for women, I think, how to stand up for something and take the heat. Sitting on the fence is the most deadening thing you can do; anyway, you don't make friends that way. You sit on the fence and then people criticize you for not making a decision.

If I could represent one thing to women, it would be to be a woman who doesn't have to necessarily choose to be one thing. If you want to bake cookies and play the drums, you can, as long as you're aware of the sacrifice and commitment. Also, you are who you are, so why not maximize it. See if all those pieces that don't fit together can fit together somehow. The personal interpretations are endless. There are women who are more creative than I am, smarter than I am. I would like to represent someone who, regardless of the degree of support, listens to her own voice instead of trying to conform to a bunch of societal rules that change every five or ten years anyway.

The bottom line is that I would like to attract people in my life whom I admire and respect. The only way I can do that is to be one of those people, too. I keep company with people who do the hard things. I wouldn't be able to hang with them and enjoy them if I didn't do that myself. And a lot of them are women. Women who laugh out loud and have no fear and ask questions and try new things—behavior that is due to the fact that they've risen to the challenges in their lives and they've won . . . and lost. They've been disappointed. They've stuck their necks out. They've worked hard. It's not just sports that do this, but sports is the only way I know.

As far as my future goes, there are some things I'd like to do in TV, but I'm not interested in forcing opportunities. *The Extremists,* for example, seemed like a good opportunity, but in the end, no. It wasn't right for me, and I have to stick to what I know is right, even if it means not doing TV, not making the money. Because I believe something better will come along. Sometimes you just want to take what's right there in front of you, but you've got to believe that if you do quality work, quality opportunities will present themselves.

I think I'm pretty good on TV. I don't mean that to sound arrogant. Because I'm an attractive female who's established herself as a professional athlete, that makes me more qualified than almost any other woman to do the kind of reporting and commentating I'm interested in. Male athletes will talk to me because I'm pretty, but I can also ask all the right questions, the real questions, because I'm a jock, too. This is a surprise to me; I never thought I'd do television. Most TV is silly, and I never imagined how I would fit into television programming. I'll never be a girl who sits behind a desk rattling off scores. I'll always be a person who does profiles or commentating. Behind every dynamic athlete is a motivation that you can't imagine. People view sports heroes as glossy, one-dimensional machines. They don't understand that the root of their achievement is real. Money and fame have distorted the truth.

I like to hope that the general disenchantment with professional sports, meaning men's professional sports, is the beginning of the growth in popularity of women's professional sports, but I'm not terribly optimistic. I don't think a decrease in interest in men's sports will translate to an increase in interest in women's sports. It's not realistic. Women don't play football—soccer, even for men, isn't popular in this country—and women's softball is interesting, but will it ever get more attention than baseball? Probably not. Women don't slam-dunk, don't play above the rim. So if people get turned off by the corruption in professional sports, professional sports will have to respond. There'll be salary cuts or something.

If there is this hunger for purity of sport, and professional sports don't satisfy it, people will start getting into extreme sports. It's already happening in kind of a dumb way. ESPN has its Extreme Games, which is ridiculous, because you can't really do extreme things in confined areas. There's no Ready? Set? Go! in extreme sports. Part of the reason it's extreme is that you can hardly get there, you can hardly film it, you can't score it, you can't turn it into some race. You come out at the end and you're alive—that means you've won.

I think women's sports will grow, but we have to be realistic about it. Until someone can find a way to make a lot of money off women's sports, they won't grow. And, as I've said, all the team sports that men play, women don't play. An exception is tennis. Women make as much as the men do. That's why I've always wanted to do a profile on Billie Jean King. She was the ONE. Not the most attractive woman, a confessed lesbian, who paved the way, getting women as much money to play as men. Twenty years ago. Are you joking? How did that happen?

The most challenging thing I'm up against now is not volleyball, but contemplating marriage and children. It's taking that emotional plunge. But you need to do that when you dream, take the plunge. It's sticking my neck out a little, which is what I do in my sport. Just by showing up to play I'm saying to the world, "I want to win." Then, when I don't, it's disappointing. But that's better than never setting your heart on anything. If you don't, you're dead anyway.

20)

Santa Cruz

SANTA CRUZ, CALIFORNIA, has a reputation for Deadheads, earth shoes, and earthquake devastation. It was the epicenter of the 1989 quake that stopped the World Series and caused the Bay Bridge to buckle. It's hot already at 9:30 A.M., not foggy, as I'd been warned to expect. No signs of fall, just the yellow blaze of late summer. Bright, melancholy weather, like smiles at a wake. Driving in on Highway 17 I pass the AIDS Awareness Project and the Homeless Garden Project. There are six-hour parking meters on the boardwalk, with a change machine conveniently located nearby.

Downtown there is a shop called Imagine, dedicated only to the Beatles, and a health food Mexican joint called Planet Burrito. No signs announcing NO SHOES NO SHIRTS NO SERVICE—too fascistic for a town where bell-bottoms have never gone out of style. When I get here I have no idea where I'm going; I just point the rental car toward the ocean—as I've learned to do throughout the summer—and trust that eventually I'll spy the giant white shampoo bottle, and sure enough, I do.

An informal poll reveals that no one is particularly happy to see the season end. One of the men's players who was picked up halfway through the season is disappointed—he is just getting into the swing of things. John, gatekeeper of the Invited Guests Section who all summer long has stared down at inaccurate guest lists, affixing red or blue plastic Bud Light ID bands to the wrists of those who could convince him that yes, they'd gone to school with Stephanie Cox, or yes, they were indeed the cousin of Liane Sato, live in Santa Cruz, and are happy just to be home. Betsy, the mother of Discus's Jennifer Johnson, says, "Sure it's been a stretch, but I'll miss this on the weekends." Jennifer Meredith says, "I'm glad this particular season's over, but I don't know what I'm going to do now—got a job for me?"

Gabby doesn't answer my question directly. She gives me one of her shrewd, narrow-eyed looks: "Let's just say this season has been *something*. If things don't change next year [meaning, if the sport doesn't change, if fours aren't released from the tyranny of corporate sponsors and opened up to franchising], I may decide to play doubles. I may get pregnant. That'll shake things up, won't it?" Doubles, of course, has been given the Olympic stamp of approval, and thus a leg up when it comes to the quest for legitimacy. Pregnancy, well, that's a frontier that few professional female athletes have explored.

Everyone is solicitous about Gabby's injury. "I've met more mothers since this happened than during my entire time on the tour!" she says.

Overheard: Kim Oden, captain of Sony AutoSound, chatting with a friend, gives the blow-by-blow on Gabby's calamity. The friend is suitably aghast.

"But what will that do to her?"

Kim O. says, "She's playing this week, or she's going to try to."

"No," says the friend. "I mean, she's a *model.*"

When Diane Shoemaker of Paul Mitchell asks about the leg and about what Gabby's plans are for the off-season—"So, will we see you on any magazine covers soon?"—Gabby kicks at the sand, "I don't think so. I'm not doing that so much anymore." Still and all and always, the modeling, the garden-variety fame, is what lingers in the minds of fans and teammates alike.

Gabby has not trained all week, nor has she practiced. Today is the first day she's played since the accident, and as to whether she'll play the entire tournament, it's game to game.

When Team Nike faces Team Paul Mitchell, who by dint of some complicated point system has already secured the league championship, they find themselves staring again at one of their former teammates, Katie Haller, who's taken captain Janet Cobbs's place for the final tournament. Cobbs is off getting married, her life resuming, intimations of life to come, when all the players will return to their off-season jobs.

A mere eight seconds into the game there's a bad call against Nike and Gabby, finding her place before the net after throwing up her arms in protest, grumbles, "I can see what kind of afternoon it's going to be already." After a half-dozen side outs there are finally points on the board, Nike 1–0. Since Charlie Brand took over in the middle of the season he's gotten brasher in his coaching, quicker to criticize, chastise, and just whine in general.

But it turns out not to be that kind of afternoon at all. They lose the game, but Gabby is playing shrewd. She's using her wit instead of her brawn, choosing wisely how to inflict wear and tear on the wound; not moving much, sticking exactly to what she does best—kill, kill, kill. Laird remarks, "Sometimes I perform my best when I'm hurt. Something about being injured keeps you from obsessing about your game."

Although this final incarnation of Team Nike—setter Chrissy Boehle, who played at the beginning of the season for Team Sony AutoSound, now replacing Julie Romius, who had to go back to med school, Jen Meredith, Christine Romero, and the injured Gabby—is lively, brasher, more well oiled, there are still the same old problems, which, for an entire summer, escaped definition. Was it lack of team chemistry? An unsuccessful combination of talents or skill levels? Or simply bad timing? Perhaps if this team had been the team that took the court back on that scorching day in May in Clearwater, Florida, all would have been different. But it wasn't, and the mystery of why one team works and one team doesn't is never solved.

The game is all tied up at 5–5 after a sand time-out taken by Team Paul Mitchell. Gabby passes by during the side change and asks Laird not to cheer while she's serving, claiming it's too distracting. Katie Haller gets in a huge kill and Coach Charlie throws up his hands and says, "There goes my don't-block-Katie-Haller theory."

Things deteriorate this quickly: It's 9–7 Paul Mitchell at 3:50 left to play; in 9 seconds, at 3:41, the score jumps to 12–7. Laird says, "Nike gets two shitty calls and suddenly it starts going Paul Mitchell's way."

Final score: Hair 15, Shoes 8.

AGAINST DISCUS NIKE BOPS out to a 3–0 lead. At 5:23 they're still up, 9–6, but Discus is sneaking back in and Nike gets that worried look. "We're ahead now, sure, but . . ."

Jen pokes the ball over—at Charlie's barking insistence. Gabby, who is otherwise playing smart and conservative, dives for a ball and lands on her knee. Eventually it is 11–6 Nike, then 13–7 Nike, and it looks as if they just might do it—but oh, how many times has it looked as if they just might do it?—but yes, yes, finally, the score is 14–8, then, on a homely little play, a dinky kill that bounces in the corner by the net, bounces off the pole, then out, Nike takes it 15–8, and their record goes to 1–1, tied with Discus and Paul Mitchell.

Halfway through the game one player's mother finds a seat next to me. She is dressed in khaki slacks, gold clip-on earrings, her fine hair blown into a bob, Junior League to the core. She watches transfixed, her lipsticked mouth slightly open as her daughter hurls herself out and over the sand, displaying one of those gravity-defying ups, a move that will be intercut into a commercial, a move that makes the game look less like an activity invented a hundred years ago to help businesswomen relax than an offshoot of bungee jumping. When her daughter lands, *umph!* stretched out on the sand, coated with sand up one side from wrist to knee, the mother clasps her hands beneath her chin. "Oh! This is so good for her!" she cries.

I find this remark curious. This, I know, is not something a man would say watching his son play sports. The father of Grant Hill does not watch his son slam-dunk and say, "This is so good for him."

"How so?" I ask. "Confidence building?"

"All of it, just all of it. It's like a One-a-Day, remember that vitamin? All the good things playing on the beach has done for her."

However far we've come in accepting women athletes, there is still and perhaps always will be a feeling that sports for sports' sake—because it's a blast to win and a drag to lose, but great, always great, to hit a ball really hard! (the only reason boys need to play)—is simply not enough for girls.

Most things written about women and girls playing sports never fail to mention how *good* it is for a girl, like eating broccoli and wearing a seat belt. Indeed, one of the most successful advertising campaigns in history is Nike's "If you let me play" series of spots, which features earnest, not-quite-beautiful little girls staring gimlet-eyed into the camera and saying things like, "If you let me play I will be 60 percent less likely to get breast cancer." This is true, and the spots are artistic and moving, but who exactly is the little girl addressing? Other nine-year-olds? What little girl says to her mother, "I want to play soccer because it will reduce my chance of unwanted pregnancy?" My own five-year-old has expressed an interest in the sport because, she says, "I like to kick things."

Of course, the ads aren't geared for future female basketball, baseball, and volleyball players. They are geared for anxious mothers with wallets full of credit cards, women who came of age before Title IX, who may or may not have tapped around a volleyball or hit a tennis ball over a net when they were fourteen or fifteen, and if they did, were certainly uneasy about it. Mothers who want to save their girls from what they fear most—self-loathing, abuse, failure. And there is nothing wrong with this. But the implication that unless a girl is bettering herself through sport, then it's not a good use of her time, won't do anything to further the acceptance of women's sports or women in sports. What will, and does, is coming out weekend after brutal weekend to watch a woman like Gabrielle Reece win, lose, and play the game.

THE NEXT DAY, Saturday, the women don't begin playing until 1:00 P.M. There is no team dinner on Friday night. Gabby is holed up in her hotel room keeping her leg elevated, everyone else more or less losing the will to find a place with good tiramisù.

Nike doesn't play until three.

The tunes at this site are the musical equivalent of Planet Burrito—Jim Morrison wailing "ya got your mo-jo workin'." The crowd is sparse but enthusiastic. Only two rows of bleachers, each three-quarters full. Watching the first women's match of the day, Sony battling it out with Paul Mitchell (the latter comes from behind to take it 13–12 by the clock), I wonder: If Nike had done better this year, if Gabby had either drafted better or the Satos had worked out, would she still feel the same way about chucking fours? She claims she needs a franchise—indeed, the sport needs to go to franchising—to succeed, and that is why she's thinking of training for doubles, or is it simply end-of-the-season weariness, disappointment, and frustration talking?

The first game for Nike, played as the afternoon breeze picks up and the air is tinged with that wistful late-summer feeling, is against Team Sony AutoSound. When the announcer introduces Liane he says, ". . . from the first family of volleyball, the fabulous Sato family. Liane Sato! Liane swears she's going to get a red card outta ya, Referee Bob-bee!" And Liane trots out and gives a thumbs-up.

Although Gabby has been playing well despite her injury, today she's not as sharp as she was yesterday. Her kills are smart, assured, and clean, but she's sagging a bit. She is spending her off-season on Maui with Laird; is some part of her already there?

The same problem that has plagued Team Nike from the very beginning plagues them until the very end—a few lousy calls, a sense that the other team is beginning to dominate, and the rallies sprint past. Serve, dig, set, kill out of bounds, point. Point, point, point. At 5:56 it's 9–6 Sony, and by 5:15 it's Sony 13–6.

The day goes long; Team Nike versus Team Norelco, Shoes versus Nubs, is the last match of the tournament and of the season. It's set for five o'clock. But at 5:45 Discus is still on the court, getting skunked by Paul Mitchell. Gabby and Laird sit with their arms around each other at one of the tables in the Invited Guests Section.

A tour official comes over with a slip of paper in his hand, ". . . your points . . ." he starts to say.

"I don't care anymore," says Gabby.

"But if Discus loses . . ." he tries again. What he means is that if Discus loses and goes down 1–3, then the outcome of the game between Nike and Norelco will determine who goes on to the semis. What he means is, "You're still in it, Gabby."

"Never mind," says Gabby. "Never mind."

He shrugs and walks away.

BY THE TIME Team Nike and Team Norelco take the sand, it's nearing six. The day is exhausted, the sun is stranded low in the sky. Even the sand, burning enough in midafternoon to require players to wear socks, is cold between the toes. Someone, somewhere, has lit a fire; the air smells of burning pine.

While Nike and Norelco warm up, Jane Kachmer and Craig Elledge sit on the edge of one of the patio tables and debate the future of the league. Jane is as ardent as Gabby is frustrated: "The sport has got to move to the next level."

"It's not time," says Craig.

"The athletes are frustrated. The sport is completely sponsor-driven and it's viewed as being less authentic because it IS sponsor-driven. It's gone as far as it can go this way. The sport has got to grow."

"All right," says Craig. "How?"

"The draft has got to change."

At that moment the whistle blows; the conversation ends.

The crowd is edgy. The bleachers are populated with people who don't have anything else to do. A gaggle of rowdy Latinos have found seats in the Invited Guests Section—this late in the day there's no gatekeeper—and cheer for whoever has the ball. The Invited Guests chairs have long since lost their lines; half aren't even facing toward the court. One guy, front row and center, is reading a book, a Bible-thick Tom Clancy novel.

All tied up 6–6 at 6:54. Christine delivers one of her monster kills. Rowdies: "YOU ARE HUGE!"

There's lots of strangled whoops, hoarse hollers, pointless dives. Both teams are hurling themselves into this; it's both sloppy and intense. Gabby is more or less stationary, due to her injury. Her kills are still accurate, but after a few murderous rallies, Team Nike does what Team Nike does best—falls apart before our very eyes. Jen tries hard, but still misses her ups. Under pressure Christine dives and kills and gets some spectacular ups, but it's her free radical approach to the sport—fierce and brainless. The ball rockets out of bounds or into the net; sometimes you wonder if she's completely clear on where the opponent is standing. Setter Chrissy is fast, but not particularly strong. Once, as Jen is trying to get there for the dig, Chrissy is in her face, shrieking: "Helpme! Helpme! Helpme!" When Jen fails to help and the ball dies, Chrissy jerks around as if she's just been shocked.

Two of the players from the men's tour are sitting near us. When Christine wipes out in yet another uncontrolled, unsuccessful dive, the guys go, "Dig the team camaraderie—no one even helps her up."

Bobby, the ref, standing at his perch beside the pole, is staring right into the low sun. He makes a huge error—thinking the ball is on one side of the court when it's really on the other, he grants a side out. Gab yells and Chrissy does her electrical shock thing, earning her a yellow card.

Rowdies: "GO TO YOUR ROOM!"

Rick, the other ref, crosses the sand to consult, and miraculously the call is overturned. Still, it doesn't do any good. Half of the court is in shadow; the chilly breeze blows; the giant white Paul Mitchell shampoo bottle, dirty white from traveling, begins deflating, sagging over the bleachers.

It's 10–10 with 3:30 left. One of the men's players wonders aloud, "Has Nike even taken third yet?" Yes, someone assures him, it isn't THAT bad. Donna Summers warbles over the sound system during a sand time-out; everyone claps; it's going to turn into a disco party.

Norelco leads 13–10, 2:01 seconds to go. There is another lunging, grunting, staggering rally to :58. The last play of the season is not as great as this rally. It's an afterthought, a piddly thing that involves Gabby trying to save the ball after one of her team members has dinked it into the net. Gabby can't dig it and it dribbles off her hands. She stares at them, these hands that once earned her $3,500 a day, as if she recognizes them, but she's not quite sure from where.

Afterward Gabby signs autographs. A woman tells Gabby that her daughter, who is already 57″ at age ten, wants to be just like her.

The once unthinkable question posed in all our heads in Detroit, in St. Louis, in St. Paul, and at all the venues on the West Coast: "Is the entire season going to be like *this?*" has been answered. Yes, it is, till the very end, it is. That night, there will be a banquet honoring the players and their season. Even though Gabby earned the most kills ever recorded in a single season, she will receive no recognition. Annette Bruckner of Team Paul Mitchell will be chosen the 1996 Offensive Player of the Year.

The good-byes are anticlimactic, like the minutes after a graduation ceremony when everyone mills around in the dusk. Stephanie Cox is in tears; her Team Discus took last place here at Santa Cruz. Walking off the beach, we pass a bunch of guys in baggy shorts playing volleyball. One of them asks Gabby how she did.

"We lost," she says.

"You can come play with us," he cajoles. "We need someone big in the middle."

"Thanks, but nah," she says. "I've had enough volleyball for now. Maybe another time."

"Next summer?"

"Sure," she says, tossing them a smile.

A WEEK AFTER the end of the season, Gabby and Laird rent a house on Maui, in the small town of Paia. The long, low house sits on a gusty point beloved by windsurfers and sailboarders the world over. The house is built in such a way that the ocean seems to surround it on three sides; sitting at the dining room table, you feel as if you are on the prow of some sturdy seagoing vessel.

Here, Gabby rests, mulls things over, waits to feel less exhausted. She rents videotapes from the tiny video shop downtown, reads, and cooks. She wanders around all day in her bathing suit and goes to bed early. The waves are disappointingly small throughout the fall and winter, and Laird has time on his hands. He teaches her how to surf.

Every so often, work requires her to fly back to Los Angeles. She has a guest spot hosting the aprés-*Tonight* talk show *Later* (formerly *Later with Greg Kinnear*), works on a new magazine column for Condé Nast's *Sports for Women,* and does a guest spot as herself on a new sitcom, *Chicago Sons.*

She goes back to the gym.

"I was discouraged, but I still think I had a decent perspective. It was like if your house has just burned down. You've just been through something terrible, but let's face it, you're still alive. I knew I'd be able to get revved up again. I was stronger. I was anxious to see how I'd be able to use some of the things I'd learned during the season. And anyway, it's just volleyball. Yes, it's life or death when you're on the court. From points one through fifteen, nothing else on earth matters, but still, the point is to play the best you can, and to enjoy yourself. I don't think I've ever lost sight of that, for which I'm grateful."

Around the new year, after continuing pressure from his players, Craig Elledge decides to abolish the draft. Gabby, as is her way, waits for a while. When the new team selection process gets under way, involving a complex rating system, and it emerges that next season's Team Nike will reunite Gabby with former teammates Stephanie Cox and Katy Eldridge, Gabby begins to feel a twinge of hope. Practice begins in March, four times a week. The season begins in May. It's a new team composed of old friends, a new season, a new chance to grind.

21

The Shoe Fits

THE IRONY IS, I've worked very hard not to be pigeonholed, not to be simply an athlete, but to do several things well. And still, I'm sort of an emblem of what the new female athlete is supposed to be. If I had it my way, the balance I've worked to achieve in my life would be what stands out and not the fact that I'm a good-looking woman who's chosen to play volleyball. Recently I read about a woman basketball player who is very tall and very beautiful and the article said, ". . . move over Gabby Reece!" and I thought to myself, *Yeah, right. I'm not moving shit.*

There are other pretty women who are more athletic than I am, but I've worked at it. I've schlepped. I've been in gyms. I've been on airplanes. I've had my worst season on record. I gotta tell you—when all is said and done, the best thing about having "made" it is that now I can finally afford to buy nice shoes that fit. If you look on the bottoms of my feet you'll see bunions the size of quarters. It's from all those years of stuffing my feet into size tens, when I really wear an eleven.

ACKNOWLEDGMENTS

TO KAREN KARBO, without whom any of this would have been possible, or funny. Thank you for your honesty throughout the project. I didn't feel like I was the only one lifting her skirt over her head. You are a special talent.

To JAK, Jane Kachmer, a godsend of a friend and a brilliant business partner. This was all your idea—do I need to get into how much I must trust and respect you?

To the coolest, smartest Red Hot Mama editor, Karen Rinaldi. Thank you for making the work great, and for all the talks we couldn't write about.

To Team Nike 96, for staying open even when it was difficult— Jen, Romero, Flea, Kim, Katie, Julie, Chrissy, Gary, and Charlie.

To Jen, Steph ("Stiff"), and Katy, for making friendship and volleyball come together. Thank you, guys, for sticking with me during the hard times as well as the great ones. I feel fortunate to have all of you in my life.

To John Francis, for your unconditional love, and for teaching me so many things about myself and who I want to be. You have been a constant ray of light in my life.

To my mom and dad, for all your gifts, and my family, the Reeces, Glynns, Boardes, and Beauchamps for all your love.

To Aunt Norette and Uncle Joe, Jose, Ron, Elyse, Peter Richardson, Connie, the Greeners, Coral Weigal, Karol and Robbie LaVie, Coach Dean Soles, Dorothy and Monta, Marianne P. from NYC, Cecile, Twanna, Cirene, Kenny "Pups" Peterson, Jeff and the Sandhoff family, Danielle Salzano, Juan Carlos,

Acknowledgments

Jay Schmalhotz, David Rehder, Lily, Dan Vrebalovich, Barbara Beirman, Holly McPeak, Gary Soto, Carol Kachmer, Phillip "P.P." Dixon, T. R. Goodman, Gilles Bensimon and *Elle* magazine, Scott Messick and MTV, *Shape* magazine, and, at Nike, Phil Knight, Tinker Hatfield, Michelle Burnett, and Lori Smith, thank you for your love, support, friendship, and guidance. There is a bit of all of you in me.

I also owe thanks to John English, Steven Meisel, Gary Nolton, Jan Sonnenmair, Sylvan Cazenave, Richard Hume, and Davis Factor.

Last, and most important, to the Chief Upstairs. To God, my creator, for this beautiful and insane gift called Life.

—Gabrielle Reece

MY THANKS GOES first to my collaborator, Gabrielle Reece, who graciously opened her life to me, and taught me how to be tall. You're a rare gem.

My thanks also go to Hampton Sides at *Outside* magazine, who commissioned me to write the article from which this book grew, and to Greg Cliburn, my editor at *Outside,* who listened, laughed, and taught me about writing.

For her candor and strength, I'm grateful to the editor of this book, Karen Rinaldi, one-time shot-putter and cheerleader. Kare—both have served you well in your job as coach, taskmaster, girlfriend, and editor. I salute you.

Thanks to my agent, Kim Witherspoon, for her unshakable faith in my writing and her take-no-prisoners approach to life and literature. A dozen roses also to her fellow players on

Team Witherspoon, in particular Gideon Weil and Maria Massie.

Double thanks to my researcher, Maria Dolan, a writer in her own right who has managed to master both the Dewey decimal system and the Internet.

Heartfelt thanks to the valiant and generous women of Team Nike, in its various incarnations, in particular, Jennifer Meredith. To quote my favorite voice in the beach volleyball crowd, "You are HUGE!"

I am grateful to Jane Kachmer, a big-hearted girl, also in the middle, who gave birth to the idea of this book, and who, like a true mother, oversaw a million details while lending love and support.

Thank you to CE Sports, for making me feel at home on the beach, especially Craig Elledge and Scott Floyd.

Thanks also go to *Women's Sports Traveller* and the Women's Sports Foundation.

On the home front, I owe thanks and appreciation to Bill and Joyce Loftis, Bill and Karen Loftis, Stephanie Loftis, and Jim and Mary Baker, for their patience, indulgence, and good humor.

I am also indebted to Marta Greenwald, Carol Ferris, Dana Joseph-Williams, Kathy Budas, and Whitney Otto, all of whom understand the woman in the writer, and vice versa.

Finally, thanks to the biggest girl of them all, Fiona Katherine Karbo Baker, the light of my life.

No writer writes in a vacuum. I also am indebted to the following writers, whose work both educated and inspired me: Holly Brubach, "The Athletic Esthetic" from *The New York Times Maga-*

Acknowledgments

zine; Mariah Nelson Burton, *Are We Winning Yet? How Women Are Changing Sports and Sports Are Changing Women;* Allen Guttmann, *Women's Sports: A History;* David Halberstam, *The Amateurs;* and Steve Rushin, "1954–1994: How We Got Here" from *Sports Illustrated.*

—*Karen Karbo*

Doing the Circuit.

Photos by John English

The girls: Stephanie Cox, Me, Katy Eldridge, Jennifer Meredith.

With Laird in Maui, 1997.

◄ **My first Nike poster.**

Photo by Richard Hume

JOE
WEIDER'S

SHAPE

May 1995

Summer? No sweat
9 steps
   to a
Beach-Ready Body

The smart kitchen
Eating well made easy

Beyond your wildest dreams . . .
Where fitness can take you

Take The China Cure Quiz
Discover your secret self
and the keys to good health

USA $2.50/Canada $2.95

Beach Pro
Gabrielle Reece

0 5

0 743458 7

May 1995

June 1995 ▶

1993